horne's

The Best Place to Shop After All

LETITIA STUART SAVAGE

THE
History
PRESS

Published by The History Press
Charleston, SC
www.historypress.com

Copyright © 2019 by Letitia Stuart Savage
All rights reserved

Cover images courtesy of Detre Library and Archives Division, Heinz History Center, Pittsburgh, Pennsylvania. Additionally, all internal images courtesy of Detre Library and Archives Division unless otherwise noted.

First published 2019

Manufactured in the United States

ISBN 9781467138352

Library of Congress Control Number: 2019948153

This work is dedicated to my research associate, William Ebner, who persisted with boxes and boxes of Horne's material while surrounded by all of the more tempting eighteenth-century treasures in the Detre Library.

Contents

Acknowledgements   7
Introduction   9

Setting Up Shop   13
From Notions to Dry Goods   23
From Dry Goods to Department Store   31
A Metropolitan Store   50
Horne's Weathers the Depression   66
Horne's Goes to War   82
Celebrating One Hundred Years   96
Horne's Moves to Suburbia   113
From Horne's to Lazarus   135
Eating at Horne's   151
Minding the Store   161
"The Best Place to Work After All"   167
Horne's for the Holidays   186
Playing at Camp Horne   209

Bibliography   223
About the Author   224

Acknowledgements

I give thanks to the following for all of their assistance:

Archivists and volunteers at the Senator John Heinz History Center's Detre Library and Archives for help identifying and accessing the Joseph Horne Company manuscripts and photographs; thank you for carrying out more than 150 archival boxes for our research and for scanning to meet our deadlines.

Those "Hornites" who donated materials now in the Heinz History Center archives and Federated Department Stores who transferred the remaining company records to the Western Pennsylvania Historical Society when they acquired the store.

The *Pittsburgh Post-Gazette* for scanning its extensive newspaper archives and making them available online. This archive provided more than 140 years of advertisements and news articles on Horne's, including material that wasn't available elsewhere. For those who would like to "shop" the stores of the past, this archive can provide hours of entertainment.

Northland Public Library, whose librarians and volunteers provided interlibrary loan services.

Avonworth Historical Society president Richard Herchenroether, who provided access to the society's information on Camp Horne, as well as images of the camp.

Avonworth community park manager Eric Shultz, who gave us a tour of the former Camp Horne, now Accord Park. The walls of the park's main building are covered with historic photographs of the camp.

Acknowledgements

Sewickley Heights History Center for background information on some of the Horne family members.

All of the people who shared their memories of the store over the years with the press and online. Each memory is a piece of history.

Introduction

At one time, Pittsburgh had more department stores than any other city of its comparable size in the country. By the time I moved to the area as a teenager, most of them were gone. From relatives, we heard stories of the late departed stores and their delights—most notably Boggs and Buhl, which was so elegant it warranted a trip from downtown across the bridge to the North Side just to shop.

But there were three major department stores left: Horne's, Kaufmann's and Gimbels. While each of them had branches in the suburban North Hills for ordinary shopping, the downtown stores had far more merchandise and more choices. Several times a year, we would make the pilgrimage into the city, especially for school clothes and Christmas gifts. These trips always followed the same route, and the first stop was always Horne's.

No one ever explained why, but there was the sense that Horne's had the best merchandise. It wasn't the most modern store. At that time, the street floor still looked like it had for decades, with its columns, soaring ornamental plaster ceiling and older fixtures. The marble stairs to the mezzanine were worn down. In the ladies' restroom, the toilets were flushed by ancient pedals on the floor, probably revolutionary when they were first installed, and you could actually sit and relax in a cozy chair.

Visiting the store was like visiting a proper, genteel older aunt who was surrounded by comfortable, gently worn things—not because she couldn't afford anything newer but because she had bought quality the first time. Horne's installed a classic interior using the best materials available and

This little girl, visiting a model play house at Horne's, is dressed up for a day of downtown shopping.

didn't succumb to fads. Customers felt the same way, and any shopper unsure about the "rightness" of either fashion or home furnishings could trust merchandise from Horne's. It was the best place to shop after all.

On our trips, we didn't stay for lunch. I'm not sure why, but it might have been the influence the coconut cake from the Tic Toc Shop at Kaufmann's had on my mother. After Horne's, we would make a quick trip to nearby Jenkin's Arcade for the pilgrimage to Parker Button and then on to Kaufmann's for lunch. We rarely went to Gimbels unless we were looking for something specific that we hadn't found elsewhere.

By the time I had graduated from college and began working, I had less time to travel downtown. I wasn't inclined to shop anyway, and the specialty stores in the small towns and local malls were easier to browse. The "uniform" skirt suits I had bought at Horne's and Kaufmann's lasted forever, and since I worked in a conservative industry, there wasn't much need for the latest fashion.

This is THE PLACE. You probably know it well, we have tried to make it well-known and well liked. It is the place to come to when you wish to get

ABSOLUTELY RELIABLE QUALITIES
and
THE MOST FOR THE MONEY.

We have been in business fifty years this fall, and in all that time we have never sold any trash—not an ounce of it.

Our Mottoes are: "Nothing but Good Goods." "No Price but the Lowest."

Fifty-six departments in the store. We sell everything from Kitchen Helps to China Bric-a-brac.

READ OUR ADVERTISEMENTS EVERY DAY.

JOS. HORNE & CO.,
PITTSBURG, PA.

From the beginning, Horne's emphasized the quality of its merchandise. This advertising card from 1899 assured patrons, "[W]e have never sold any trash—not one ounce of it."

When Horne's spiraled into a slow decline and eventual closing, it was almost like watching the final years of that genteel aunt. Shoppers did not realize what they had lost until the store was gone. I was probably one of them.

Horne's advertising policy, articulated in the 1920s, captures its culture. It was to be "sincere and dignified and strives to give interesting information regarding the store, its merchandise, and services. Comparative prices are used with restraint." Advertising emphasized fashion and the sensibleness of merchandise, not the price. In the early days, there was only one store-wide sale per year, and clearances were limited.

There was no Sunday advertising at the time, "a policy which respects the Sabbath observance convictions of the founders." Additionally, "The store does not…raise its window curtains on Sunday.…While today the public attitude has considerably softened on this subject, the Joseph Horne Co. feels that many of its customers still appreciate this condescension to the seventh day. The same rule applies to working on Sunday. No employees are permitted in the building on Sunday except watchmen, and others required for safety and building maintenance."

And yet Horne's was in no way backward. It was the first store in Pittsburgh to send its buyers abroad to select merchandise and the first to abolish evening openings so its employees could work shorter days. It was the first store in the city to install pneumatic tubes to replace cash boys as the public protested child labor. Many of those cash boys were apparently assigned to other jobs in the company; years later, long-term employees of the store remembered starting as cash boys. Horne's was the first store to motorize its delivery system, the first to install a telephone ordering board and the first to embrace both radio and later television, broadcasting fashion and home furnishings programs. Ironically, it didn't protest when cross-town rival Kaufmann's claimed some of these "firsts."

Even in its final days, Horne's held to its standards as best it could in a changing retail environment. It was still the place for fashion, operated one of the premier bridal salons in the city and decorated lavishly for the holidays. When Horne's closed on Christmas Eve 1995, it bequeathed its final gift to the city: the giant illuminated tree on the corner of its building. The tree is still lit at the start of every Pittsburgh holiday season.

Setting Up Shop

In 1846, Pittsburgh was a bustling town, rebuilding itself after a disastrous fire the previous year had destroyed one-third of its buildings. It was already a center for manufacturing, with iron and glass factories lining the banks of the Monongahela, Allegheny and Ohio Rivers. For a young man eager to make his way in business, Pittsburgh meant opportunity.

Twenty-year-old Joseph Horne recognized that opportunity and left his family farm in Napier Township, Bedford County, for a job clerking in a store owned by Mr. Yeager. He soon left for a similar position working for Lorenzo Eaton, who owned a store at 63 Market Street stocked with trimmings and fancy goods. According to his contemporaries, Joseph Horne was a hard worker and had a knack for the trimmings business. After three years, Mr. Eaton offered him a partnership; Mr. Eaton may have been considering retirement at the same time. Joseph Horne bought out his partner's interest in the business in 1849 and renamed it Joseph Horne & Company.

Two advertisements in the *Pittsburgh Daily Gazette* on February 22, 1849, documented the event. The first announced, "Co-Partnership. Lorenzo Eaton & Co., have this day associated with themselves Mr. Joseph Horne, and the business will hereafter be conducted under the style of Joseph Horne & Co., at the old stand No. 63 Market, between Fourth Street and the Diamond." (The "Diamond" referred to Diamond Street, which is now Forbes Avenue.) The second declared that the "Joseph Horne & Co. have on hand a large and well assorted stock of Trimmings and Fancy Goods, to which they invite the attention of the city and country trade. No. 63 Market St."

Joseph Horne bought out partner Lorenzo Eaton in 1849 and opened his own trimmings store, seen in this artist's rendering, on Market Street, center of commerce in Pittsburgh.

Joseph Horne was only twenty-three when he opened his first store, selling to retail customers and, through the wholesale business, to other retailers. His first store on Market Street was small, just eighteen feet by sixty feet, but the building included three stories and a basement. The retail business occupied the first floor at street level, and the wholesale business occupied the upper two floors. Around 1849, the store had twelve employees and sold approximately $111,000 of merchandise each year.

Joseph Horne & Company was not a typical dry goods store at this time. It didn't carry fabric, the mainstay of the dry goods business. But trimmings were big business when fashionable women's dresses were ornately decorated with braid, ribbons, tassels and lace. One dress could require yards and yards of trimming. Sewing machines had recently been invented, and more women were sewing for themselves at home. The store carried innovations like newly available sewing thread on spools rather than flat cards. Joseph Horne & Company also sold hoop skirts, bonnets and some men's clothing like underwear.

An advertisement in a Pittsburgh directory for 1852 published by Woodward and Rowland described the business:

> *Joseph Horne & Co*
> *Wholesale and Retail Dealers in*
> *Trimmings, Lace Goods, and Hosiery*
> *Combs, Buttons, Threads*
> *Gents Fine Shirts and Furnishing Goods*
> *N. 77 Market Street*
> *Pittsburgh*

Six years later, a small advertisement advised, "Our excellent stock of French Embroideries and the low prices at which they are marked, offers inducements to ladies wishing to purchase the latest styles. Joseph Horne." The restrained language would be a hallmark of Horne's advertising into the next century.

In the 1850s, businesses selling dry goods and similar products were centered on Market Street between what was then known as Third Street and Fifth Street. Horne's neighbors included Cooper's "Mourning Goods" next door, Orr's Trimming Store, Robb Boots and Shoes, Stevenson the Jeweler, Mentzer Dry Goods, Hess & Wegeforth Dry Goods, Don Fraehlich Dry Goods and James Goslin Plumes, Ribbons, Ladies Hats and Bonnets.

One of Joseph Horne's neighbors who met him in 1850 had worked at A.T. Stewart Company in New York, a leading dry goods retailer. In 1914, he said that Joseph Horne reminded him of A.T. Stewart in the quiet way he conducted business:

> *How often I have seen Mr. Horne in the wholesale building devoted to that*
> *part of the business. When he came in the front door word soon reached*

every part of the building announcing "Mr. Horne is in the building." And
I have seen him afterwards conferring with the partners in the business, no
doubt giving his advice as to what should be done.

Pittsburgh was growing rapidly in the years before the Civil War. Railroads were expanding, and plank roads improved transportation. The city added horse cars in 1859 so people from residential areas could come into town to shop. Joseph Horne's business prospered as Pittsburgh grew.

In 1860, Christian Bernard (C.B.) Shea joined the company as a partner to handle finances so Joseph Horne could concentrate on buying. The growing business also needed more space. On June 4, 1862, Joseph Horne & Company expanded into a similar building next door, advertising its location as 77 and 79 Market Street. (At some point, the building numbers were changed, but the store hadn't moved.) The two buildings were still not big enough to accommodate the business, so additions were made at the back. Additional wholesale space at 75 Market Street was leased.

During the Civil War, Joseph Horne & Company employed eleven people. An 1863 advertisement listed its merchandise and the necessities of the day. They included "collars, sets, and sleeves"; ladies' dresses at the time had removable collars and detachable white undersleeves. Customers could buy linen and lace handkerchiefs, corsets, bead nets and sun umbrellas to protect delicate complexions, as well as red, white and blue neckties and Union cockades. The store carried "ladies & children's undergarments." In 1865, it advertised summer underwear for gentlemen, including "gauze and gossamer vests and drawers."

During the war, the business was challenged as prices skyrocketed. An employee later remembered that prices for muslins increased from six to eight cents per yard to forty cents per yard, as did the prices for calicos. Prices for cotton goods doubled and then tripled and quadrupled.

The employee also remembered that the store sold hoop skirts by the case since all fashionable ladies wore hoops under their dresses. Hoops were often stiffened with lengths of whale bone or cane. While fashionable, they could also be impractical both for the wearer and those around her. First of all, they took up a great deal of space; a hooped skirt was often four to six feet wide. They didn't compress easily. If a lady backed into a wall or a crush of people, pressure on the back of the skirt would raise the front, immodestly revealing ankles or even a lady's petticoat and drawers.

On April 23, 1864, Joseph Horne & Company advertised a "new and great invention in hoop skirts" in the *Pittsburgh Gazette*. The skirt was

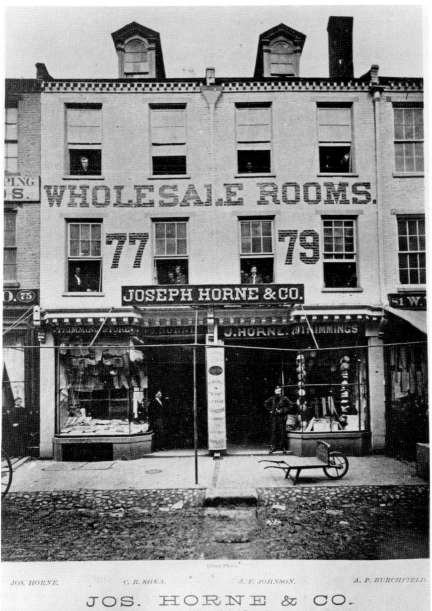

Joseph Horne was so successful that he and his partners expanded their business in 1862 into two buildings, nos. 77 and 79, on Market Street. Notice the wheelbarrow, used for deliveries, in front of the building.

made with steel springs, "enabling the wearer in consequence of its great elasticity and flexibleness to place it and fold it when in use as easily and with the same convenience as a silk or muslin dress. It entirely obviates and silences the only objection to hoop skirts, viz: the annoyance to the wearer as well as the public especially in crowded assemblies, carriages, railroad cars, church pews or any crowded place." The ad promised, "A lady having enjoyed the pleasure and comfort and great convenience of wearing one of the Duplex Elliptical spring skirts for even a single day will never afterwards willingly dispense with them." Presumably, Horne's sold these improved skirts, called caged crinolines, by the case too.

Joseph Horne & Company continued to expand after the Civil War. Joseph Horne's cousin Albert Horne, who worked for the company for decades, started his career as a seventeen-year-old on April 12, 1865. Lee had surrendered three days earlier, and the whole country was rejoicing. Albert remembered:

> *I came to Pittsburgh on April 12, 1865. I left home on the eleventh and came from Somerset to Johnstown in a stage coach. I had never seen a locomotive and was on the platform of the Johnstown station when the train came in. I was 17 years of age and I never saw anything that was so wonderful and surprising to me as that locomotive. We stopped at the Mansion House on Liberty Avenue.*

Joseph Horne wasn't in Pittsburgh when Albert Horne arrived, so C.B. Shea assigned him to work in the notions department, the foundation of the business. When the boys who worked in the store asked him where he was rooming, he told them "two tootie two Tin Pot Alley" so they nicknamed him "Tootie." Albert recalled his first meeting with Joseph Horne in an interview with an author writing a history of the store:

> *"My first sight of Mr. Joseph Horne was on Friday morning, about seven o-clock, at which time the store opened," he remembered. "I had never seen him and he had never seen me, but he knew me and said, 'You are Albert*

By 1865, Joseph Horne was the model successful merchant and a respected Pittsburgh businessman.

Horne.' I will never forget how he looked. I had read a book when I was a little bit of a boy, which was called, 'The Successful Merchant,' and he looked just like the man described in that book. He wore a Prince Albert coat and a silk hat and he had side whiskers."

On Sunday evening, April 14, 1865, President Lincoln was assassinated in Washington, D.C.:

"On the morning of the fifteenth, I do not think I have ever seen so dark a day as that morning and before noon the town was draped in black." Albert recalled. "Every yard of black goods in Pittsburgh was bought up—black calico, linings, and muslins. From a state of great hilarity, the country was in a spasm of grief. On Monday, the store closed at eleven to one for services in the different churches."

He went to church but hurried back before everyone else and was assigned to clean the corset department for the remainder of the day:

The son of a man whose store I was in in Somerset had been in a store in Dayton, Ohio. When I was coming to Pittsburgh, he told me that very likely I would see everyone running to the doors to see the parades but for me to stay back of my counter and attend to my business. After the first week I was in the store, bands went passed [sic] the store for the soldiers coming home. Everyone rushed to the door but I stayed at my counter. Mr. Joseph Horne came along and said "Albert, why aren't you at the door with the others?" I answered "That is not my place. I am paid to stand back of my counter and attend to business." He said, "Is that the way you feel about it, Albert?" I said, "Yes, sir. That is exactly the way I feel." He replied, "If that is the way you feel about business, you will succeed." That was the first feather in my cap.

One of those returning soldiers was Major Albert Pressley Burchfield, who had worked for Joseph Horne as a boy before the war. He left the store to join the volunteers but rejoined the firm as a partner in 1865 to direct the wholesale business. The Horne, Shea and Burchfield families would manage the company into the next century.

Although the store on Market Street was small, it carried a wide variety of notions and "fancy goods." Gloves, embroideries, laces and men's "furnishings"—shirts and ties—were on one side of the store. Clerks sold men's furnishings from two counters with four feet between them. From the center square, customers could buy hoop skirts and balmoral skirts. The balmoral skirts, popular during the Civil War, were made up using about four yards of fabric and featured horizontal stripes that encircled the skirt. On the other side of the store were the notions, hosiery, yarn and zephyr, a yarn blend of wool and silk. The store also sold untrimmed millinery and ribbons. It opened at 7:00 a.m. and closed at 6:00 p.m. on weekdays but stayed open until 9:00 p.m. or 10:00 p.m. on Saturdays. Like all retailers at the time, Horne's was closed on Sundays.

One of Horne's early shoppers remembered the Market Street store in a 1930 letter to Mr. Burchfield, descendant of the major and then president of Horne's:

> *I accidentally came across your* Modes and Manners *for February and also the picture of the first store. I can remember when a little girl, going there with my mother, as she would not buy anywhere else but there. I can remember it was a long, narrow store with one long counter. And on the other side of the store were shelves piled high with goods.*

At the time, shoppers did not select their own merchandise from displays. Instead, clerks would bring items from drawers and shelves for them to examine. Selling required thorough knowledge of the stock and ability to "read" the customer. Prices for items could vary based on what the clerk thought the shoppers would pay, and sellers and buyers could negotiate a price. One businessman later identified Joseph Horne as a man of progressive ideas who originated the concept of "one price" in Pittsburgh. Every item had a single price no matter who was buying.

Although most of the shoppers at the time were women, the clerks were men. Once a sale was made, clerks wrote out the checks on small slips of paper about three inches square. The check included the sale number and the amount of the sale. The checks were then given to the store cashier. In 1867, a two-part check was introduced; one part stayed with the store and the other part was given to the customer. In 1869, the George B. White Company introduced a printed sales slip, which Horne's adopted.

Individual clerks did not handle money at the time. If a customer wished to pay cash, the cash and the slip were taken to the cashier, who recorded the sale and made change. Often the money was carried by "cash boys" who ran between the selling floor and the cashier's office with a customer's money and returned with change. Clerks did record charge sales in a book kept at the rear of the store. Charge customers were billed twice a year, in January and July. Charging privileges were not easy to get, and charge customers had to have exemplary credit.

In addition to selling, clerks took turns decorating the windows. "The window displays were something marvelous," Albert Horne remembered. "Everything was hung in festoons."

At the time Horne's opened on Market Street, much of what would become downtown Pittsburgh was still residential. People still lived in houses on Penn Avenue, and anything beyond Smithfield Street was considered "far out of town." To serve residential customers, Horne's added a delivery service in 1865. Robert Tocus, the store porter and a former slave, delivered packages by wheelbarrow. When demand increased, the store hired Noah Struthers, and the company had two wheelbarrow delivery men. When Mr. Tocus retired in 1919, age eighty-six, Horne's was making deliveries by truck.

By December 1867, according to an article in the *Pittsburgh Commercial Gazette*, Horne's was a shopping institution. "The exterior of the building is modest and unpretending," the reporter commented. "The first floor is deep and commodious, and is filled with one of the richest assortments of goods ever exhibited in this city." The firm had apparently expanded the first-floor selling space when it acquired the building next door, since the article described the store as 30 by 120 feet, with all of the goods organized by department for efficient shopping. It was staffed by fifty "ladies and gentlemen." "They are polite and obliging to customers and always prompt to wait upon them, never deeming it irksome to show goods. Some of them have been connected with this house for many years…so that purchasers are sure of dealing with experienced persons."

Horne's operated its retail and wholesale businesses from Market Street until 1872. The wholesale side of the firm was much larger, selling between $500,000 and $600,000 worth of merchandise annually, while retail sales accounted for $75,000 to $100,000. Horne's had wholesale customers from all of the towns surrounding Pittsburgh and had managers who handled these customers by region. A.P. Burchfield was still managing the wholesale side of the business, while Joseph Horne was the primary buyer for the merchandise.

Pittsburgh continued to expand after the Civil War, and the population had doubled by 1871. Horne's was also growing and needed still more room. On January 24, 1871, the retail store moved to Library Hall at 197–99 Penn Avenue, while the wholesale business remained at Market Street.

Joseph Horne operated a wholesale business on Market Street until 1872 as "Jobbers of Ribbons, Silks, Millinery Goods, Straw Hats and Bonnets, Velvet Ribbons, Trimmings & Ornaments, White Goods & Lace Goods at New York Prices."

With more room, the retail business could add additional stock, including dry goods, and in its elegant new surroundings, it began to develop its reputation as Pittsburgh's store for the "carriage trade." A store history later noted that Joseph Horne had high principles, selected high-quality wares and insisted on high standards of service, all of which attracted the "better elements of Pittsburgh."

From Notions to Dry Goods

B y 1871, the city of Pittsburgh was twice as large as it had been when Joseph Horne opened his shop on Market Street. There simply wasn't enough room at the original store to accommodate the shoppers who flocked there. There wasn't enough room to expand the retail operation on Market Street either. Store managers decided to move the retail store several blocks north to Library Hall on Penn Avenue. The new store opened on January 24, 1871.

In some ways, it was a bold move. At the time, many people thought that splitting the business and moving the retail operation away from the Market Street commercial district was a bad idea. They expected the retail business to fail. The first sale at the new location, six spools of cotton thread at $0.06 per spool, might have supported their predictions. But by the end of 1872, sales totaled $250,000; by 1882, they were $1.25 million.

Library Hall was a relatively new building, constructed in 1847 of brick with a plain sandstone front. It first housed Mercy Hospital and then the Thaw Library, hence its name. Patrons could reach the Bijou Theater through one of its four entrances. The Roosevelt Hotel was later built on the site.

Horne's occupied two floors in Library Hall. Each selling area measured 24 feet by 160 feet and was fitted out with elegant, carved black walnut furnishings. The store had 150 employees, many of whom were cash boys who carried money from the clerks to the cashier's office.

A fountain in the center anchored the first floor. The mail order department, an important component of the retail business, was on a balcony near the

To find more room for his expanding business, Joseph Horne moved his retail store to
Library Hall on Penn Avenue on January 24, 1871. Detractors said that it was a mistake to
leave the Market Street commercial district.

fountain. At the right of the store near the corner display window were the
lace curtains and draperies; men's furnishings were to the right of the center
entrance, notions were to the left and yard goods were to the right of the
next entrance. Brass hardware was near the curtains. A stairway led to the
second floor.

On the second floor, Horne's sold ready-to-wear clothing and millinery.
The ready-to-wear clothing included dress lengths that Mr. Horne bought
in New York or abroad. They could be made up for customers in the store.
Children's things, which also included some ready-to-wear clothing, were at
the extreme left of the second floor at the second window. The credit and
bookkeeping offices were also on the second floor. According to employees
who worked in the Library Hall store, the third and fourth floors of the
building were not occupied.

In addition to the selling floors, Horne's leased the wooden-floored
basement. The receiving and delivery departments were in the basement,
and employees remembered how unpleasant the area could be after a flood.
Packages to be delivered were passed through a window onto Penn Avenue.

Joseph Horne had decreed that no packages be brought out of the building after 6:00 p.m., but the night watchman sometimes broke that rule so that items could be picked up for the 8:00 p.m. express delivery.

With more space, the store was able to expand its stocks. In 1875 and 1876, it added its first dry goods, the fabrics traditionally sold in dry goods stores. Albert Horne remembered that the first fabric offered to retail customers was ten pieces of Bonet silk that sold from $1.50 to $5.00 per yard. Soon Horne's was selling muslins, calicos, woolen dress fabrics, domestic linens and lace curtains. In addition to fine lace to decorate clothing, shoppers could find lace shawls that sold for as much as $500, as well as imported hats, gloves and French perfumes. High-end dress fabrics like silk and wool were also imported. There were regular exhibitions of imported French hats.

Fabric was a huge business at a time when women's dresses were made of yards and yards of material. Those who could afford it employed dressmakers to make clothing for them, but they often chose and bought their own fabric. Horne's became known for its wide stock of choice fabric and knowledge of fashion. It added special-order dressmaking to its services during the late 1870s and became renowned as an upscale dressmaker.

An advertisement of the time illustrates the breadth of Horne's fabric offerings: "For Wedding Costumes, we offer a large line of Elegant Brocades, Duchesse Satin, Ottomans and Comtess, in cream and pure white tints, with pearl garnitures and real laces to match." The ad listed colored dress silks,

With more space in Library Hall, Horne's began carrying fabric, the mark of a typical dry goods store. This advertisement, printed at the bottom of a silk program for events in the Library Hall theater, lists fabric among Horne's merchandise.

flannels and black silks: "Our Mourning Black silks in Venetians and Armurs are the very best." And there were the dress goods: "Two sides of our one large room is crammed full of Cashmeres and French All-wool Fabrics; too many kinds to speak of in detail."

Horne's also began selling coats, cloaks and suits, the first ready-to-wear clothing for women, from the Library Hall store. They were so popular that an additional storeroom next door was added. Albert Horne recalled that he sold the store's first sealskin sack, a type of fur coat, during the 1870s. Twenty-four inches long, it retailed for between $125 and $150.

By 1877, the store had twenty-two departments and had begun to manufacture the mattresses, window shades and upholstered furniture that it sold in its store. Pillows and bed ticks were filled with feathers in the store's workrooms. Horne's was open from 7:30 a.m. to 6:00 p.m. Monday to Saturday, with the men's furnishings department staying open until 9:00 p.m. to accommodate professional men who would shop after leaving their offices. The store closed at noon on summer Saturdays and was always closed on Sundays so employees and shoppers could celebrate the Sabbath.

At the Library Hall store, Horne's embraced many of the innovations sweeping the retail industry. Between 1879 and 1889, it added electric arc lights to supplement the gas lighting and, in 1885, the first telephone. An automatic pneumatic tube system was introduced to supplement the cash boys. New merchandise was introduced twice a year in what were often called "Grand Openings." One opening in the spring featured the newest fashions in time for Easter, and a second opening in the fall was timed to debut fall fashion and merchandise for Christmas.

While the wholesale business initially stayed on Market Street, Horne's needed more space as it grew. In 1881, the store's wholesale business moved to a large building at Wood Street and Liberty Avenue that the local press described as a "Palace." It had wood-paneled walls, steam elevators, a ventilating system and five floors of merchandise, as well as the largest plate glass windows west of the Alleghenies. Although Pittsburgh was a center of glass making, the windows had been manufactured in France. Joseph Horne's wholesale business was now earning $2 million per year.

While Horne's embraced some new retail technologies, it continued to do business as it had on Market Street. The bookkeeper worked in a small room with no windows, where he made out all of the accounts in longhand. They were mailed to customers every three months. While Robert Tocas and Noah Struthers still worked at the store as porters, they no longer ran the wheelbarrow delivery service. Instead, the two wheelbarrows were

Joseph Horne and his partners had a building constructed at Wood Street and Liberty Avenue to house the wholesale business. The building had steam elevators and the largest plate glass windows west of the Alleghenies.

"propelled by husky boys." One delivery route ran three times daily across the river to Allegheny, where it was a "familiar sight to see the gleaming Horne's wheelbarrows with packages tied to them moving along Ridge, Lincoln, Western, and Allegheny Avenues."

The second route ran in the city, with customers on Penn Avenue, Duquesne Way and the cross streets between Third and Tenth. Some of the best customers lived on Wylie and Center Avenues as far as Dinwiddie Street. The delivery boys liked to run packages as far as the 500 block of Wylie Avenue because they could make extra money. They were given fares so they could take their wheelbarrows on the horse cars, Pittsburgh's primary public transportation at the time. The horse cars were reliable but slow; a boy pushing a wheelbarrow could walk faster. The boys could pass on horse car transport, deliver their packages faster on foot and pocket the fare—ten cents on the uphill part of the ride and five cents on the downhill.

By 1885, wagons were delivering Horne's packages to Oakland and Lawrenceville twice a day. Packages for Shadyside, East Liberty and Homewood were delivered to Union Station, where customers could pick them up.

By 1885, Horne's had augmented its wheelbarrow delivery with single horse delivery wagons that could reach "outlying areas" like Oakland and Lawrenceville.

By the time later rival Kaufmann's opened its doors across town, Horne's was well on its way to capturing the "carriage trade," as upper-class shoppers were known. Its advertisements were discreet, with restrained language. It never advertised in the Sunday papers and installed curtains in its show windows that could be drawn on Saturday night so that Sunday window shoppers would be forced to respect the Sabbath.

While shoppers could ride the new horse cars into town to shop at Horne's, many now arrived in private carriages. They were greeted by a doorman, and the horses and carriage were taken to the Red Lion Stables behind the store to wait while the owners shopped. Coachmen could opt to exercise the horses instead, driving them along Penn and Liberty Avenues. In one version of the store's history, an observer noted "the delight of the young people of the neighborhood to whom watching the 'carriage trade' at Horne's was as impressive as opening night at the opera."

Among the "carriage trade," Horne's became a mecca for fashion. Not only did Joseph Horne travel to New York and Paris to buy for the store, but the head of the dressmaking staff also traveled to Paris twice a year to bring back designs that would be copied by dressmakers in the store. Special-order dressmaking became an important store service for those accustomed to hiring a dressmaker. More adventuresome women could combine Horne's fashion expertise and high-end imported fabrics to create their own custom clothing at home.

When she retired in the early 1930s after fifty years of service at Horne's, Mary Agnes McCully remembered what she described as the "Elegant Eighties." She had started working at the store as a fourteen-year-old cash girl and eventually became a buyer, as noted in an article from a Pittsburgh newspaper on her retirement:

> *"I think they were dressier in those days," she said. "The women had more time to choose their clothes, and they thought nothing of standing two or three hours for fittings. Of course, they used to faint, but we always had some good strong smelling salts to revive them, and they'd be up on the fitting stand again. Oh, I tell you, they had stamina in those days."*
>
> *"And the dresses and coats and furs that they wore!...Why, not a dress went out of this store that wasn't all lined in silk, and coats and capes were trimmed with ermine, sable or sealskin."*
>
> *"There was Mrs. William Thaw, for instance. Her clothes were gorgeous. I don't think anyone nowadays could hold a candle to Mrs. Thaw in her prime. She bought hundreds of dresses every year—not only for*

herself, but for young girls she knew, school girls she would be helping in her quiet way. Nothing cheap about the clothes either and in those days you couldn't touch a good dress for less than $50."

"I wish I had a dime for every sailor suit I've fitted Pittsburgh girls into when they went east to school. They wore plain blue Peter Pan outfits of two or three pieces. And they looked mighty neat, too. Nowadays young things going away to school, insist on a trousseau a bride would envy. But back in the days when the best families drove up in their broughams for a day of shopping, young girls were kept pretty much in the background. Not until they were eighteen or nineteen did they get anything very elegant in the way of clothes."

By the end of these Elegant Eighties, Horne's needed still more selling space. Like many other dry goods stores across the country, it had developed into a new form of retail: the department store. From its dry goods roots, it had learned to appeal to women, especially the middle- and upper-class women who would redefine shopping as a leisurely urban pastime. No longer content to just shop, women wanted a place to meet friends, eat in a safe female enclave and be entertained. For them, Horne's was ready to build what historians would later call a "Palace of Consumption."

From Dry Goods
to Department Store

B y 1890, it had become clear that Horne's needed still more space for its retail business. The Industrial Revolution was fostering a new population of consumers eager for the latest products, and dry goods stores across the country were evolving into a new form of retail: the department store.

By the end of the century, Victorian clothing for women—with its complicated construction and yards of fabric—was passing out of fashion. Women were embracing the blazer suit, a long skirt with a matching jacket similar to a man's coat. Suits were practical and allowed women to walk on the street without attracting attention; they could also avoid rude comments from men. By 1900, suits were the mainstay of women's ready-to-wear clothing, and almost every woman who could afford a suit owned at least one.

The immense popularity of the shirtwaist expanded the ready-to-wear trend. Introduced in the summer of 1892, it was an immediate hit. A fitted blouse with a high collar and long sleeves, a shirtwaist could cost as little as thirty-nine cents and could be worn with either a skirt or with a blazer suit.

Dry goods stores responded to the demand for women's ready-to-wear clothing and expanded their suit and cloak departments. Since suits were easier to make, some stores manufactured their own ready-to-wear; others bought ready-to-wear clothing from manufacturing centers like New York. Simpler styles meant that clothing could be made in factories by immigrant tailors and seamstresses.

Some historians believe that the rise of women's ready-to-wear clothing was the engine that transformed the old-fashioned dry goods store into the department store. Dry goods stores had sold ready-to-wear clothing for men—it made up 70 percent of the available ready-to-wear clothing in the 1890s—but ready-to-wear clothing for women transformed the retail industry.

Horne's had leased additional space on Penn Avenue to expand its suit and cloak department, but it was clear that the store needed to expand further. In the past, the business had always rented retail space. Now the managers looked down Penn Avenue and acquired the plot of land at its western end at the intersection with Fifth Avenue (later Stanwix Street). They planned to build a new store, a "Palace of Consumption."

The articles of incorporation filed for this business show the scope of their plans "to establish and conduct a general department store." The document not only included a list of the items it was already selling—furniture, china and glass, utensils, stationery, meat and provisions, drugs, jewelry, plated goods, perfumes, toilet articles, items for recreation, newspapers and books and musical instruments—but also services it could offer. It could employ hairdressers, restaurant keepers, nurserymen and florists, photographers, printers and engravers, "dealers in domestic trained and fancy animals," tailors, dressmakers, furriers, milliners, hatters, glove makers, boot and shoe makers, house decorators, engineers, real estate agents, contractors, cabinetmakers and upholsterers. Whatever the shoppers of Pittsburgh desired, they could find at the new Joseph Horne Company.

Sadly, Joseph Horne, the company's founder, did not live to see the grand plans come to fruition. The new store was under construction when he died in October 1892. A Pittsburgh newspaper commented, "His name has been associated with the progress and prosperity of western Pennsylvania for many years. A man of strict probity, as well as large business understanding, it was natural that he should build up the immense interests that were carried under his name and direction for so long." The article continued later:

There are few business men in Pittsburgh whose names are known so well in the home as that of Joseph Horne. Hardly a lady goes out for an afternoon's shopping without a visit to Horne's being on her program and most Pittsburgh women knew the courteous, white-haired gentleman who, until the commencement of his fatal illness, could always be found during business hours in his retail stores. The respect and esteem that have always been entertained in this community for Jos. Horne are the cause of general regret at his exit from the stage of business and philanthropic life. He left behind him the businessman's greatest treasure—the monument of an honored name.

By the late nineteenth century, Pittsburgh residents no longer needed to confine their shopping to small general stores or specialty shops. Most cities boasted a new form of retail: the department store. In New York, A.T. Stewart had established what would become the three main principles of modern selling that would define the department store: one price, rapid stock turn and a departmentalized organization of goods to be sold.

Since each item had a fixed price, there would be no haggling, and stores could hire inexperienced clerks, which reduced their labor costs. All shoppers were welcome and could come in and browse the goods. The store, usually a multi-floored building in a central city location, offered customer services like restrooms, delivery, package wrapping and credit.

The first floor of the new Horne's store at Liberty and Stanwix included ornate walnut fixtures. Merchandise was kept in drawers or behind counters, and clerks showed items to customers. Shopping took time; notice the stools at the counter for the customers.

Many stores really were palaces. The first floor, where the store established its identity, often featured marble floors, large columns, a first-floor mezzanine and wide aisles. Stores sold higher-priced impulse items on the first floor and moved merchandise that shoppers would purposefully seek out to the upper floors. Fabrics, for example, which had dominated the first floors of the dry goods stores, were moved to upper floors. Hydraulic elevators, which replaced stairs, allowed shoppers to easily reach the upper floors.

Joseph Horne & Company officially opened its new building on July 31, 1893. At the time, the managers announced in a newspaper article, "Our sole aim is to make it as near as perfection as possible...its occupancy will mark a new era in retail merchandising."

The new store, designed by W.S. Frazer, was built on a steel framework faced with Oolitic limestone on the first story; the five upper stories were brick and terra cotta, with copper cornices and molding at the windows. There was a large skylight in the roof. The building had its own dynamos and boilers for steam and ten thousand feet of steam pipe and seventy-five radiators to heat the store. A flood protection system was installed to keep water out of the basement during Pittsburgh's frequent high water. The building cost $700,000.

Inside, the mezzanine floor set the tone. It was 120 feet by 25 feet and "richly furnished; it is devoted exclusively to the use of lady visitors." A ladies' parlor provided a place for women to rest between bouts of shopping. Five Otis hydraulic elevators were installed to carry passengers to the upper floors, and a freight elevator ran from the basement to the sixth floor to carry stock. Elevator enclosures were ornamental bronze.

The store also featured the latest lighting technology. Horne's had been one of the first stores in Pittsburgh to use arc lamps instead of gas lamps. Gas lamps not only created fumes and heavy shadows but also required constant maintenance. In the evening, the floor walker would have to count the number of lamps lit and tell the lamp trimmer who cleaned the chimneys in the morning. He also had to report the numbers to the gas company, which billed according to the number of lamps lit. With 240 arc electric lights and 200 incandescent lights, the new Horne's was modern, bright and gas free.

A new pneumatic tube system, the first in the city, supplemented the army of boys who ran cash and packages throughout the store. There was a restaurant on the sixth floor and a bicycle school on the roof. A personal shopping service was available to assist customers, and the store's shirt sales were famous across the region. Not only did local shoppers flock to

Horne's was one of the first stores in Pittsburgh to install a pneumatic cash tube system in 1893 to supplement the "cash boys" who carried payments from customers to a central cashier.

the new Horne's, but people from across the country also visited to tour the latest building innovations.

Three years later, the magnificent building was totally destroyed. Late one Sunday night, a barrel of waste paper and trash spontaneously combusted in the basement of T.C. Jenkin's wholesale grocery warehouse at Penn Avenue and Cecil Alley. The night watchman discovered the blaze and poured buckets of water on it to extinguish the fire, but he wasn't successful. The fire roared up the large freight elevator to the roof of the building. An alarm was sounded just after midnight on May 3, 1897, and soon multiple fire companies from the city and nearby Allegheny were on the scene. It would be the largest fire in Pittsburgh since the 1877 riots.

The fire in the grocery warehouse was fueled by hundreds of barrels of lard and sugar. In spite of the firemen's best efforts, the building was soon a "tornado of flame," as a newspaper described. The firemen abandoned it and tried to save the surrounding buildings.

According to press reports, the wooden window frames on the upper floors of Horne's caught fire first. "The two watchmen in Horne's store, as soon as it was discovered that the cornice of the top floor was on fire collected all the Babcock extinguishers and loaded them on the elevator, rushed them to the top floor." The newspaper reported on Monday morning, "These, with such volunteers as they could muster, they turned loose, and for a while did noble work, but the heat was too great and they were compelled to leave."

Soon the entire store was engulfed. A witness described the sight to a Pittsburgh reporter:

> When the flames broke out of the Jenkins building and swept across Penn Avenue to Horne's store the glass from the windows in that building fell upon the sidewalk like hail. I cannot liken the fire in the Horne building to anything that would afford a better illustration than a burning stubble field in autumn. I have seen a field of stubble catch fire and sweep in irregular billows. When the fire got into the Horne building the flames licked up the fine silks and other goods, jumping from one table to another. It was an interesting as well as an awful sight.

The fire, visible from houses on the hilltops of Allegheny and the South Side, drew hundreds of spectators, who crowded the streets to watch. At one point, the store's horses, hitched sixty feet away, were panicked by the rising heat and broke loose, running through the crowd. No one was seriously hurt. The heat also affected the hoses and fittings on the fire engines parked in the street, and they had to be moved.

At 1:30 a.m., firefighters and spectators were startled by the first of several explosions from the Jenkin's basement, where oil was stored. The explosions

Following a May 1897 fire that started in A.C. Jenkin's grocery warehouse, the new Horne's store was reduced to a shell. Business losses in buildings and merchandise totaled $2 million.

broke plate glass windows in the area and further weakened what remained of the grocery's walls. One wall collapsed, burying and killing a young fireman. Several other firemen were injured.

The next morning, what remained of Horne's was still smoldering, and the streets were blocked by rubble. The store's total losses were almost $2 million; the fire had consumed the Horne's office building as well as the store and its contents. More than a dozen other businesses and residences were also destroyed.

Horne's managers, as prudent businessmen, had insurance to cover their losses. Before the steel skeleton of the old store was cold, they had leased the nearby Phipps Building and sent buyers on a special train to New York to purchase new stock. The Phipps Building was new but had been damaged in the fire. Three crews worked around the clock to repair the fire damage and install fixtures and merchandise in the temporary store. It opened on May 17, 1897, two weeks after the disastrous fire.

Horne's managers also planned to rebuild the old store. "As soon as the ruins are cold we will begin work on a new building," said Joseph O. Horne. "We will have the debris cleared out as fast as a big force of men can do the work," he continued, "and then will go to work on the new building."

The fire may have been a blessing in disguise for Horne's. As the press reported, the original store was thought to be large enough when it was first built, but the business was expanding so rapidly that it needed more room. The fire had destroyed the store and the Horne's office building, as well as other structures in the area. The managers now planned to build a larger store encompassing the entire square from Penn Avenue and Stanwix Street to Cecil Alley. It opened in 1898.

A second fire in April 1900, possibly started by faulty wiring, damaged the reconstructed building and resulted in a $758,093 loss. Horne's used the opportunity to hire Boston architectural firm Peabody and Stearns to design a Beaux-Arts exterior for the building and was back in business within a month.

Four years later, when a Pittsburgh newspaper described the store, Horne's had clearly returned to its former glory. The writer found the mechanical systems in the basement interesting (he started his tour there): the boilers, dynamos, the big pumps that powered the elevators and the blower that forced air through the pneumatic cash carriers. The rest of the basement was retail space for the household department, cheap grades of cotton, plain linens and cleaning supplies. It also included what was called the "bargain exchange," where departments sent sale merchandise.

The basement was clean and efficient but far from elegant. "We step into a waiting elevator and instantly find ourselves on the main floor. What a panorama meets ones eyes! What a lofty room, 23 feet from floor to ceiling." Multiple aisles filled the vast space, each one lined with counters and shelves for goods. Clothes for ladies were on the second floor and clothes for children on the third. The impressive millinery department was also on the third floor: "Here one sees case after case of French plate glass in which are displayed every new and stylish bit of feminine headgear simultaneously with its first appearance in Paris, London or New York. A lady here can have the advantage of walking down long aisles on both sides of which are shown thousands of stylish hats ready to wear, and untrimmed ones and the trimmings all ready to be made up to her order by the nimble fingers of the scores of skilled milliners in the work rooms in the rear of the department. Altogether a millinery show room unequaled anywhere."

Following a fire in 1900, Horne's hired a Boston architectural firm to upgrade the exterior of the store, as seen in this 1903 image.

The upper floors of the store were devoted to household furnishings—furniture, curtains and interior design services on the fourth, a massive Oriental rug gallery and fine china on the fifth. Mail orders from around the country were also handled on the fifth floor; the store issued a large catalogue twice per year for its mail-order customers. On the sixth floor, merchandise from around the globe was unpacked and sent to the sales floors below. There was also a kitchen and dining room for the employees.

The writer reveled in statistics—the forty large windows on each floor, the huge sixth-floor skylight, four hundred feet of street frontage on Penn Avenue and Fifth Street and the 240 arc lights and 200 incandescent lamps that lit the store. It was hard to believe that Horne's had been totally destroyed by fire less than a decade earlier.

Horne's faced a different challenge in March 1907. On March 15, the Ohio River crested at 38.7 feet, and Pittsburgh, Allegheny and the surrounding region flooded. The water was 5 feet deep on Penn Avenue in front of the store. Because they were only blocks from the Allegheny River, the store managers had prudently installed a flood protection system as the store expanded. Steel flood gates had been installed over the show windows and entrances, but they weren't enough to protect the store. As

39

This early advertising card shows Horne's after the devastating fire of 1897 and after Pittsburgh acquired the final *h* on its name, circa 1907.

the water began to rise outside, employees built a barricade around the store and used pumps night and day to remove the water between the barricade and the store. Horne's was the only building in the flooded area of the city to remain dry.

Because of the flooding in the street, the store had been closed on Wednesday, March 14. Apparently, it opened the next day, but shoppers had to "venture over by way of our Penn Avenue bridge." The next day, an advertisement in the *Pittsburgh Daily Post* declared, "We hope to be in touch with the mainland to-day." Another ad in the *Pittsburgh Sun* clarified that there would be no wet goods on sale at Horne's—other stores in the city were selling flood-damaged goods cheaply—because the water hadn't come into the store.

In spite of the challenges of fire and flood, Horne's continued to expand. In 1903, the East Building was constructed, and the store occupied the entire block on Penn Avenue from Cecil Way to Fifth Avenue.

For those who had the leisure to shop—primarily upper-middle-class and upper-class women, the store was truly a Palace of Consumption. Women could browse the latest fashion, find household necessities from linens to porch furniture, choose elegant gifts of china or silver for brides and attend

When Pittsburgh rivers flooded on March 15, 1907, water was five feet deep on Liberty Avenue in front of the Horne's store. Heroic efforts by employees kept the water out of the store.

entertainments like fashion shows and product demonstrations. If they tired, they could rest in the tastefully appointed lounge; if hungry, they could eat with friends in the tearoom, safely separated from men.

In the late nineteenth and early twentieth centuries, department stores presented their new merchandise to shoppers at biannual "openings," held in the spring and fall. An article in the local press described a typical spring opening at Horne's in 1892: "Paris millinery at its best and brightest, all selected personally by the representative of this house, made a bright and spring-like picture that told of sunshine to come."

The article went on to describe the wonders throughout the store:

On the second floor parlor of the cloak room the exquisite array of Paris costume, capes and tea gowns were surrounded by groups of admiring beholders, who could fully appreciate the artistic draperies, and true Parisian deftness of design so charmingly shown in the elegant and striking display which brings the best efforts of Paris workroom of world-wide celebrity to the easy and comfortable inspection of the ladies of these cities. Quite cute and pretty are the novelties shown in the adjoining room devoted to the wants of young girls and small children, including the wee little ones, the latest comers to the family.

There were boys' suits in "styles exclusive to this house. The fact that their children's clothing is made to order in the most perfect manner and newest ideas is a matter of some importance to ladies who formerly paid extravagant prices to Eastern houses for inferior service."

The store was brightened with a colorful parasol display: "Paris parasols, of course, to make a correct tout ensemble with the Paris bonnets and Paris costumes."

Horne's openings were major events after the turn of the century. Gertrude Gordon, feature writer at the *Pittsburgh Press*, described a fall opening in October 1910:

In a maze of marvelous millinery, gorgeous gowns, magnificent furs, and with flowers and potted plants and rippling fountains everywhere, the autumn fashion opening of the Joseph Horne Co. began this morning to continue three days. At every entrance on the first floor of the immense department store, and placed with an eye to the artistic effect throughout every part of the store are great pyramids of plants, autumn leaves and fresh flowers. Each department is given over to the newest, the freshest, and the best materials and articles pertaining to its own particular division.... On the second floor has been arranged a stage, decorated with palms and flowers and a pretty little electric fountain. Here pose the models brought to Pittsburg from New York in order that Pittsburg women may have every advantage of viewing the new gowns.

After a detailed description of several outfits presented on the stage, she addressed the hats, essential to every woman's outfit at the time: "In the millinery department are carriage, auto, walking, suit, dress, afternoon, reception, wedding, morning and evening hats ranging in style through every effort of the New York milliners' imagination, and in price from that afforded by the most modest purse to breath-taking expensiveness. A feature of the opening is the display of ready-to-wear French mourning millinery, which is a novelty in Pittsburg."

Four years later, a Horne's advertisement for the "Spring Opening" focusing on new dresses commented, "The fact that Pittsburgh women are interested in the world's best fashions is all the incentive we have needed to provide the best fashions of the world." Prices for the dresses ranged up to $165 and suits to $200. A later ad advised, "We have assembled new, smart modes for every demand of the well-dressed woman—home, street, matinee, luncheon, dinner, dance and the more formal evening occasions. We invite your personal inspection of the new features revealed by this beautifully complete and varied showing. Its interest is heightened by our close personal relations with Paris, which assures styles to the last degree."

The store continued biannual openings as late as 1917. With the focus on French fashion, Horne's cemented its reputation as Pittsburgh's fashion authority, a reputation that it had already held for decades. Store letterhead from the time shows three addresses: Pittsburgh, New York and Paris.

Like most department stores of the time, Horne's relied heavily on newspaper advertising to attract shoppers. While the store refused to advertise in the Sunday papers, it did advertise throughout the week and often ran multiple ads in a single edition of a local newspaper. When Horne's was located on Market Street, the ads were un-illustrated lists of merchandise and prices. Now the advertising language continued to be restrained—no shouts for attention here—but the store added illustrations, usually simple, elegant line drawings of upper-class activities like travel by ocean liner or train, entertaining or "sea bathing." By April 1914, Horne's was using the tagline "The best place to shop after all" in its advertising. Another line, "Style…The Store Supreme…Service," appeared at the same time, often as a banner across the top of larger advertisements. Horne's also identified itself as "The Modern Store" in some advertising.

The advertisements provide a window into the consumer world at the beginning of the twentieth century and the lifestyles of the typical Horne's customer. There were all of the things needed to stock the well-run late Victorian house: linens, rugs, curtains (including parterres to hang between rooms), cut glass, silver vases and china, including Haviland. A large advertisement in September 1915 notified shoppers that a large shipment of "interesting Japanese things" had arrived for those who wanted kimonos, silks and tea sets. The store was manufacturing and upholstering its own furniture and making mattresses, pillows, draperies and awnings. With all of the things to buy, it is no surprise that sales of consumer goods roughly tripled between 1909 and 1920.

Selling furniture in addition to fabrics was often the first sign that a dry goods store was becoming a department store. Early factory-made furniture was often considered shoddy and badly designed. Old families still relied on inherited antiques or custom-made furniture to furnish their houses, but the newly rich industrialists in Pittsburgh didn't have much to inherit. Instead, they could rely on Horne's. In an early advertisement for its annual furniture sale, the store advised customers, "Everybody should shun 'cheap' furniture—it's too dear for anyone who has to count the cost, and too shiny to suit good taste. Whatever furniture we sell you is the best of its class—this store has never had anything of a shoddy nature since it was founded 58 years ago—and it never will."

Ready-to-wear clothing was also becoming a department store staple. By 1915, women's ready-to-wear clothing was dominating some Horne's advertisements, with the store identified as the source for "Style Supreme." While some of this clothing was probably purchased from manufacturers, Horne's was advertising locally for sleeve makers, skirt makers and waist makers, so it may have been providing some ready-to-wear clothing made in house. In addition to clothing for women, the store also sold ready-to-wear for boys and girls in a separate children's department.

Sportswear was also appearing on the scene, both for participants and spectators. Horne's used tennis terms to advertise its wide array of tennis clothing in an ad headlined "Tennis Toggery." The toggery for tennis included silk sports jackets and regulation striped blazers, sweater coats, sports dresses and suits (proper women wouldn't dream of appearing in pants) and silk stockings in fifty different colors.

In the winter, skating was very popular at Pittsburgh's Winter Garden, and Horne's declared, "As the Style Supreme Store of this city, it is our pleasure to invite you to an inspection of correct and distinctive attire specially designed for skating wear." There were skating dresses with muffs and hats to match, fur-trimmed velvet and corduroy suits, sweater coats, knitted scarves, skating caps and hats and velvet muffs with a deep pocket designed to hold a skater's shoes. Of course, under it all a woman skater required a corset designed for freedom of movement, and Horne's advertised these as well.

Horne's had served male customers from its early days on Market Street. Now, as department store shopping was filling the store with women, it recognized the challenge that might be for men. Men had their own department, with a separate outside entrance so that they could shop efficiently without being delayed by gaggles of women in the store aisles.

An advertisement from 1916 shows a clearly successful businessman being dropped off by his chauffeur. While Horne's had sold men's ready-to-wear underwear and shirts for years, it now sold suits, advising men that there was little difference in quality between their ready-to-wear suits and those made to measure by a tailor. "If a coat or a vest or a pair of trousers need some alterations to make them fit WE HAVE AS EXPERT TAILORS AS ANY SHOP IN TOWN, AND CAN ALTER CLOTHING SO THAT ABSOLUTE PERFECTNESS IN FIT IS GUARANTEED."

Horne's daily advertising reflected assumptions about its customers: that they followed Paris fashion and had lifestyles that required an extensive wardrobe, that they had the leisure to play tennis and take up skating and could afford to spend forty-five dollars for a skating suit, that they were accustomed to visiting a tailor for made-to-measure suits and that a chauffeur would deliver men to the store to shop. In 1911, the store advertised a large sale of cotton fabric, "especially for those who must have an entire wardrobe ready before starting for the seashore." There was an assumption that children went away to school, often in the East, and that girls, as well as boys, were headed off to college. In September 1917, the Horne's Misses Shop was advertising its experience in selecting wardrobes for school with the headline "College Girls Are Packing Their Trunks."

Horne's also assumed that its customers traveled beyond the seashore. An advertisement in May 1913 noted, "When one 'goes to Paris' one always takes a number of commissions for friends. 'Bring me some Undermuslins,' is a frequent request, made by a friend who little realizes that right here at Horne's The Very Things You Would Purchase are displayed, and sold at prices that do not make worth while the trouble of bringing them back." ("Undermuslins" was the discreet term that the store used for ladies' underwear.) Several months later, Horne's opened a Liberty Shop on its fourth floor because "Travelers in Europe have brought interesting tales of the wonderfully curious and novelty merchandise which Liberty of Paris and London have on display." Shoppers were advised that they could find scarves, lengths of fabric, tapestries and cushions for early Christmas gifts.

While Horne's managers understood that they were catering to a wealthier clientele, they didn't just assume that their shoppers would spend carelessly. Even the richest had worked hard for what they had, and the industrial elite came from a culture that valued frugality and careful use of resources. In an interesting advertisement of the time, the store declared, "When Buying Something Good, Why Not Have the Best?...said a prominent business man, who brought his two daughters to the August Fur Sale, the opening day for a new coat each. 'There are many price baits held out to you to buy things just because they are cheap; but it is better to pay a little more, if necessary, and get something that you can be sure will give you real pleasure and lasting satisfaction.'"

Quality and value, not cheap prices, would be at the core of Horne's selling philosophy. That didn't mean that it excluded all but the rich. "This store is for everybody—regardless of pocketbook—who appreciates merchandise of the standard this store set for itself long years ago, and has steadfastly maintained," the store stated. "While this store specializes in the finer grades of merchandise, much of it is moderately priced, well within the means of all, today."

Horne's shoppers were not just interested in the latest fashions. Technological innovation was changing the way that people lived in the early part of the century. The store had embraced innovation like telephones and elevators in its own buildings and offered the latest technologies to its customers. It had a separate Kodak department for photography enthusiasts; during a 1907 demonstration of film development using Velox paper and light, customers could bring their own film and have it developed free of charge.

By 1915, Horne's was selling electric fixtures and appliances. An advertisement for "Electric Week" just before Christmas explained, "From Atlantic to Pacific, the Nation is blazing with electrical enthusiasm. Electricity is being talked about as perhaps never before. It is a movement to forcibly show people the many advantages and the many uses to which electricity can be put, not only in street-car lines, automobiles, and street lighting, but in the home. Joseph Horne Co. has long featured electrical appliances for the home." The advertisement then listed appliances on sale: electrical irons, toasters, chafing dishes, nursery milk warmers and heating pads, most of which were made by Westinghouse. Perhaps ironically, the advertisement also listed a special sale on flashlights.

Horne's did not just assume that its customers were rich enough to have electrified their houses and could buy electrical appliances. In the middle of a streetcar strike in May 1919, it advised customers that they could use the telephone ordering service, assuming they had installed telephones at home. "You are no farther from Horne's than you are from the nearest telephone." It also knew that many customers did not have to rely on mass transit. "Shoppers who come to town in their own machines" would find a "parking lot reserved for Joseph Horne Co. shoppers."

Department stores didn't rely solely on advertising to get people to visit. Stores became centers of entertainment, hosting product demonstrations, special events and exhibits. In 1915, Horne's advertised an exhibition of china making and reminded readers that there were always interesting things going on in the housewares department; it was "necessary for you to stroll through every few days if you don't want to miss something." For the children, the store started an annual Doll's Tea Party, where little girls could bring their dolls to the store and have tea in the restaurant without hovering parents. During the event, there were activities for boys who came with their sisters and favors to take home. The girls received the cup and saucer that they drank from. The store's toy buyer had purchased three thousand cup and saucer sets during a buying trip to Europe to choose Christmas toys. Parents were required to order tickets for the event and wait outside the tearoom to pick up their daughters when the tea party was over. It was wildly popular.

For those who couldn't travel for the coronation in London in 1911, Horne's displayed a copy of the queen's dress, cape and overdress with long train that she would wear at the ceremony, along with a copy of the crown and staff. In a Friday store advertisement in November 1915, Horne's listed the events at the store for the next day. Cooking and baking in glass dishes would be demonstrated in the glasswares section of the third floor, shoppers could see how to clean silver without polishing and the opening for men's bathrobes and smoking jackets would take place in the haberdashery department.

Entertainment extended to the store windows. Glass could now be made in large sheets, and large plate glass windows were standard in modern department stores. With the rise of fashion, windows were important to attract customers. A souvenir booklet for the Pittsburgh Exposition in 1892 included a photo of a large white elephant made of linen and lace that may have been in one of Horne's windows; using handkerchiefs for elaborate window displays was common at the time. Later, a "Projectscope" was used in one of the windows to demonstrate how Ronseard kid gloves were being made in the United States. When Horne's decorated the main rooms of the new William Penn Hotel, the sketches were displayed in one of the store windows.

Store services were also key to a store's popularity. By the first decade of the twentieth century, Horne's had added a children's haircut shop, fur storage and a restaurant with "Special Lunches for Busy Men and Busy Women." For either thirty-five or fifty cents, busy men and women could enjoy a complete lunch of beef short ribs, cold tongue, broiled halibut, chicken croquettes or veal with vegetables, pie or ice cream and coffee or tea. Customers were advised that "our wagon will call" for furs, rugs or any other item requiring cool storage for the summer. Horne's promised, "We will insure them against moths, fire, and burglary. When alterations or repairs are made on furs at the request of the owner, where charges amount to $20.00 or more, no extra charge will be made for storage."

Package delivery was a critical service for a department store; if shoppers were encumbered by packages, they were less likely to keep shopping.

Make Yourself At Home On the Balcony

Make use of the many Services at hand

Personal Service Bureau	Children's Barber Shop
Silence Room	Writing Desks
Charm Shop	Check Room
Ask Mr. Foster Service	Shoe Shine
Telephone Booths	Retiring Room

JOSEPH HORNE CO.

This advertising card from the early 1920s outlines the balcony services available to Horne's shoppers. On the balcony, they could find telephone booths, a check room, the Children's Barber Shop and the Ask Mr. Foster travel service. For exhausted shoppers, there was also a "Silence Room" and a "Retiring Room."

Shoppers could have their packages held at a special desk as they shopped and collect them before going home or they could simply have their merchandise wrapped and delivered to their homes.

While Horne's had initially used wheelbarrow boys and a single horse-drawn wagon for delivery, it now had a fleet of shiny two-horse wagons. Initially, the horses were stabled close to the store at Penn and Second Street. Hay and straw were kept on the third floor; the "barn boss" lived on the second floor, where equipment was also stored; and the horses were housed on the ground floor. The store also had a stable on the North Side at Reedsdale and Frazier (later Fontella) Street.

While horses delivered packages in the city, packages to Beaver, Sewickley and other "outlying parts" were delivered by train. At the local stations, subcontracted horse and wagon teams picked up the packages and delivered them to customers' homes.

Horse and wagon delivery was a big expense since stores had to feed and care for horses and maintain and repair wagons and harness. Horne's had a fleet of one hundred wagons when it added its first motorized delivery truck in 1903. The truck, a Conrad two-cylinder steamer, was the first for a department store in Pittsburgh. Store employees remembered how noisy it was. It was replaced by two-cylinder gas Oldsmobiles.

By 1910, Horne's had a fleet of White trucks. Motorized department store delivery was still so unique that a 1911 advertisement for White trucks in *Scientific American* featured a Horne's delivery truck. By 1918, all of the Horne's delivery horses and wagons had been replaced by motor trucks. In 1919, the store made its first long-distance truck delivery, hauling a load of fine furniture to New York. The delivery team of drivers and a mechanic made the eight-hundred-mile round trip in six days.

In 1916, Durbin Horne, who had succeeded his father as president of the store, died, just six months after retiring. He had been actively involved not only in the business but also in the professional life of Pittsburgh. Joseph B. Shea, son of C.B. Shea, became president; Horne's was now being led by the third generation of the founding families. Albert Horne, who had joined the firm in 1865 and left in 1882 to start a mercantile business, had returned in 1906. He had met with Durbin Horne because he was contemplating a career change and said that he was thinking of going to New York. "Don't you think of it," Durbin Horne had told him. When Albert Horne asked him for advice he said, "Well if I were you, I would come back to this store." Although he had been a competitor of sorts, Albert Horne was welcomed back and brought with him thirty-six employees who also joined Horne's.

By 1919, Horne's was well positioned to prosper in the next decade. Store facilities had been upgraded in 1916, and Horne's joined other national department stores to form the Retail Research Association and the Associated Merchandise Corporation. While stores retained their independence, these professional organizations allowed them to address national retail issues and cooperate on buying to secure lower prices from manufacturers. With World War I hampering trade with Europe, Horne's sent its buyers to the Far East to investigate manufacturing opportunities there and place orders.

When the economy roared in the 1920s, eager shoppers would find whatever they wanted at Horne's.

A Metropolitan Store

Many historians contend that the 1920s marked the high point of the department store industry. Society was changing quickly, people were becoming less economically conservative and they had lots of money to spend.

Some of the most radical changes happened in women's fashion. Women were rejecting long hair for daring "bobs"; they were shedding their long skirts, multiple layers, confining corsets, dark stockings and high shoes. Fashions were changing so quickly that stores had to send their buyers to New York many times each year just to keep up. By January 1921, Horne's had formed a close relationship with New York fashion magazine *Vogue* and had a *Vogue* room on the store mezzanine; in newspaper advertisements, it reminded shoppers that Horne's was the only department store in the city carrying *Vogue* patterns for home sewers.

While spring and fall "openings" had persisted in conservative Pittsburgh, they had fallen out of favor in other cities. Soon even Horne's, one of the most conservative stores in the city, had abandoned openings to bring out fresh merchandise throughout the year.

Fashion in the 1920s had changed radically from that of a decade earlier. The waistline dropped to the hip, and the hem rose almost to the knee. The clothing was looser than it had been and didn't need to be fitted by a dressmaker or experienced home seamstress. This meant that it was much easier to manufacture. Higher-quality, respectable ready-to-wear clothing lured the middle classes to department stores. There was still no standard

While this Horne's fashion window from the 1920s features hats, the white tennis dress worn by the model shows how radically women's clothing had changed in the 1920s.

sizing and stores incurred high costs in alterations and returns, but ready-to-wear clothing had become a department store staple. Sales of ready-to-wear clothing now exceeded fabric sales.

Women were also wearing more jewelry. In the late nineteenth and early twentieth centuries, many women wore no jewelry at all, and those who did often wore nothing more than a discreet brooch. Now "costume jewelry" became the rage—ropes of beads, chunky bracelets and novelty pins. Before 1894, only women with pierced ears could wear earrings, but the invention of the screw back allowed any woman to decorate her ears. By 1922, Horne's was advertising earrings as "Novelties"; many of them were dangles with "some extreme ones almost to the shoulders."

Women were also beginning to wear make-up. In 1900, respectable women might wear a touch of powder, but that was all. In the 1920s, department stores began selling higher-end cosmetics. In March 1921, Horne's was the only store in Pittsburgh selling Elizabeth Arden "Toilet Preparations," and by summer of 1922, the store was selling powder and rouge, along with its other "Toilet Goods" like soap and hand lotion.

American women were also wearing perfume. Returning World War I soldiers had brought gifts of French perfume home with them, and now women clamored for it. In October 1925, Horne's also introduced Chanel fragrances to Pittsburgh, and French perfume became a standard in advertisements for women's gifts.

Department stores had struggled to maintain merchandising ties with Europe during World War I, but after the war, Paris was still important as a source of fashion. Now almost all of Horne's buyers were making annual trips to Europe. In September 1924, the store advised its customers "Paris Brought to Pittsburgh"; it had eighteen buyers traveling there for merchandise. Horne's described its Paris office as "one of our most active foreign offices. Through this office come original models from the famous couturiers and modistes as well as all manner of apparel, accessories, and luxuries for the home."

The results were available to Horne's shoppers. In November 1925, those who were able to move south for the winter or who planned a winter trip were told:

> As smart Parisians are being made ready for a season on the Riviera, smart American women are considering apparel for warm climates not only on this continent but those in all parts of the world.... Our showings of apparel for tropical and semi-tropical climates are very inclusive.... They consider southern cruising... They consider those who take up winter residence in Florida or Southern California.... They consider tourists to Bermuda, the West Indies, Cuba, the Orient. Not only has all the apparel received its inspiration from the same source as that which will be seen at points along the French Riviera, but the showing includes many garments which we have imported direct from Europe's fashion centers.

Clothing for those headed south for the winter was also featured in the store magazine *Modes and Manners*, published bimonthly for its customers. Its Christmas 1924 issue included fashion predictions for Biarritz, a "gay French resort," and how those predictions would foreshadow fashion at Palm Beach and the California resorts.

In addition to Paris, Horne's had offices in major European cities to source merchandise for the store. The London office focused on men's clothing, "sport togs," sporting goods, woolens, linen and pottery. The office in Brussels focused on linen, art needlework and beaded bags and the Florence office on Venetian glass, damask, brocades and coral cameos. There were additional offices in Germany, Czechoslovakia and Switzerland. During the war, Horne's had started buying trips in the Far East to find alternative sources for items it had bought in Europe. Now it offered embroidered lingerie, negligees, dressing gowns and kimonos from the Philippines, Japan and China. In 1929, the store announced that it was opening a Rowe of London Shop in the boys' clothing department to give Pittsburghers access to "famous outfitters to the children of British royalty and aristocracy."

Sportswear for participants and spectators became more popular in the 1920s, as people had increasing leisure time and money to play. Horne's not only sold golf clothing and equipment for men and women, but it also employed a golf "pro" to give lessons. Women still played in dresses and skirts, but they were buying "athletic corsets" and lightly boned athletic girdles. (By 1920, Horne's was selling bras as well as traditional corsets.) The store also sold wool and linen riding habits; tennis and golf sweaters, skirts and coats; and tennis, golf and riding blouses. There were also "Motor Coats—sturdy coats intended for the modern feminine occupation of driving one's own car."

And if driving one's own car wasn't challenging enough, there was flying. In 1929, at the same time Horne's was displaying the type of airplane Amelia Earhart was flying, it held "An Exhibition of Flying Clothes and Accessories for Women and Men" in the Sportswear Shop. An advertisement described the people who might be interested in the event: "a debutante bent upon learning to handle the controls so that you can taxi about in your own plane as you now drive your roadster…a man going to play aeroplane golf this Spring…a woman planning a flight to California…a business executive with the idea of hopping by plane from one branch of your firm to another."

While most Pittsburghers weren't likely to take up flying, swimming was popular. The long, heavy woolen bathing suits of the early twentieth century were evolving into shorter, lighter suits. They were still made of wool but now exposed a woman's arms and legs. Horne's advertised practical Annette Kellerman suits, as well as "Beach Costumes of Satin, Taffeta, Foulard and Silk Poplin" that could cost as much as $125.

The modern bathing suits exposed much more skin, and women were no longer afraid of being in the sun. In 1929, the store employee magazine, the *Horne-Pipe*, described how the new "sports mode" fashion for a suntan began a few years earlier in France and had spread to the United States. The low backs of fashionable dresses would allow a woman to flaunt her tan. To help customers coordinate their summer tans with their wardrobes, Horne's

During the 1920s, women were embracing sports like golf. These players at Camp Horne may have used their employee discounts to purchase their sportswear at the store.

offered a new service. A woman could have the back of her bathing suit cut to any shape so that it would match the backs of her dresses.

Customizing bathing suits was not the only new service that Horne's provided. During the 1920s, department stores learned that store services could increase sales. They could lure people to the store, increase the time that they spent there and make shopping easier and more satisfying. A shopper might drop off a dress for alterations and be tempted to look for matching accessories. She might stay in the store for lunch. Credit plans would allow her to buy new furniture without having to save for it first.

By 1921, Horne's had a Doll Hospital in the store, and parents were encouraged to bring in favorite dolls so that they could be refurbished for Christmas. The next year, it added the popular "Ask Mr. Foster," a nationwide travel and information service. "Mr. Foster" would eagerly help customers plan their trips, reserve Pullman and ship accommodations, purchase tickets, engage rooms at hotels and "give cards of introduction." The service was free. Horne's also started a hosiery repair service that was so popular that people from across the country sent their damaged stockings to the store. There employees operated special machines to repair runners and snags in silk stockings; by 1929, they were repairing seven thousand pairs of stockings per year.

Store credit remained a popular service. Horne's did not use the term "credit" but instead noted that "convenient payment may be arranged" for furs, furniture and radios. During the annual furniture sale, a store advertisement assured customers, "Our Department of Accounts has arranged a plan of deferred payments whereby responsible persons may extend payments for Furniture purchased during the Sale over a period of months. This plan will greatly facilitate matters for young people who are just getting to housekeeping and who wish to conserve their finances as much as possible." Of course, store credit was limited to "responsible persons," generally those of the upper and solidly middle classes.

During World War I, Horne's managers had decided that they needed to expand their store, but the war made that impossible. In 1921, during the postwar depression, they began the expansion. They were lauded in the local press for letting contracts to local firms in the middle of the economic downturn. Local architect Benno Janssen designed the expanded store, and Mellon-Stuart handled the construction. The steel for the project came from American Bridge Company in Ambridge and the brick from the Kittanning Brick Company. The electrical engineering staff at Carnegie Institute designed the electrical control panel using the latest technology.

The "new Horne's" increased the store's selling space by 65 percent to almost sixteen acres, cost $2.4 million and took two years to finish. Eight stories tall, it extended Horne's along Stanwix Street to Duquesne Way. The *Pittsburgh Mercantile* newspaper declared that it was one of the finest stores in the country.

In the basement, the store had its own power plant to provide steam for heat and electricity for light and power. The flood control system was upgraded, and 100 percent of the store was equipped with automatic sprinklers. There was a completely new ventilation system; fresh air would enter the store through iron louvers at the tops of the show windows and be heated in the winter. Ten additional elevators were installed—seven for passengers and three for freight—with electrical equipment provided by Westinghouse.

The freight elevators were connected to an upgraded shipping and receiving area on Duquesne Way. There eighteen trucks could be loaded or unloaded under cover on a work platform that extended for 120 feet across the back of the building.

To reflect the growing importance of store services, a new service balcony extended across the rear of the store above the main floor. The services here were not restricted to customers. A traveler spending just a few hours in the city could check his luggage, freshen up in the restroom or barbershop, send a telegram, get railroad tickets and make Pullman and hotel reservations at "Ask Mr. Foster" or meet friends. The balcony also included telephone booths, a hairdresser and manicurist, an optometrist and a shoeshine stand.

The expanded downtown Horne's store opened to the public on April 24, 1923, and thirty to forty thousand people attended the open house.

Horne's did not just expand its downtown store. It still needed more space for workrooms and storage, and in April 1927, it announced that it would be building a new warehouse on the North Side at the north end of the Manchester Bridge. The new warehouse would have eight floors and a basement and was estimated to cost $2 million. The new warehouse would consolidate operations from five warehouses across the city, including the one not far away at Reedsdale Street.

Before the new warehouse was completed, tragedy struck. An Equitable Gas storage tank as high as a ten-story building and so large it covered an entire city block exploded on November 15, 1927. The force of the blast destroyed Horne's Reedsdale Street warehouse and the merchandise inside. Two employees were killed in the explosion, and another employee was killed the next day when he was doing salvage work at the site and a floor collapsed. Twenty-five other people were killed and almost one hundred were wounded when nearby factories and houses were destroyed. The blast blew ten- and fifteen-foot steel girders four blocks from the tank and broke thousands of downtown windows. Total damages reached $5 million.

Horne's managers had prudently purchased explosion insurance during World War I, and it covered the financial losses from the blast. An advertisement on December 10 reassured the public that damaged merchandise had gone to the insurance companies and that none of it would be sold to the public.

Horne's new warehouse opened on November 16, 1928. Designed to be fireproof, it was constructed of reinforced concrete, finished with tapestry brick and trimmed with tile and sandstone; it also included an extensive sprinkler system. Inside were Horne's workrooms, stockrooms and storage vaults. The workrooms had facilities to make window shades, awnings and curtains and repair furniture, upholstery and Oriental rugs. Its freight elevator could lift twenty thousand pounds and could take a fully loaded truck to all of the eight floors. There were additional elevators for people and merchandise.

A 1928 booklet produced by the store announced "Horne's New Cold Storage Vaults the Most Modern in America." The new warehouse included

By the 1920s, Horne's had a fleet of delivery trucks, including larger trucks for delivering furniture and smaller trucks for packages.

The sports illustrated on this scoreboard advertising Horne's Men's Store—polo, tennis, golf and fly fishing—reflected its well-heeled clientele.

dry cold storage vaults for twenty thousand furs. Horne's would pick up customers' furs for storage and re-model them before the next season.

While Horne's still relied heavily on advertising to draw shoppers, it also embraced new communications technologies, including radio. According to Westinghouse Electric and Manufacturing Company, the store was instrumental in the development of KDKA, the first commercial radio station in the country.

Westinghouse had been experimenting with radio after World War I, and its assistant chief engineer, Dr. Frank Conrad, had set up a transmitting station in his house. His audience of radio enthusiasts, mostly teenage boys, listened in on sets they had built themselves.

In its toy department, Horne's stocked kits and parts for making wireless sets. It also set up a wireless receiving station in the department as a demonstration and advertised it "for the accommodation of our patrons, and any who are interested—particularly small boys, or the young men who were in the radio service during the war, and who haven't had an opportunity to 'listen in' for some time—are invited to come in and use the set, without obligation. In the afternoon there is usually great activity in the air."

One evening, when toy department employees were working late, they listened on the receiving station and heard a twenty-minute broadcast of Victrola music transmitted by Dr. Conrad. The next morning, they told the advertising department what they had heard, and the head of advertising sensed an opportunity. With the headline "Air Concert 'Picked Up' by Radio Here," he used the event to advertise wireless sets.

A Westinghouse vice-president saw the ad and decided that there might be a market for a commercial station to broadcast to the public. It established KDKA. The station's first broadcast on November 2, 1920, provided election results and announced Warren G. Harding's presidential win.

In January 1921, Horne's advertising manager, looking for new publicity opportunities, contacted Westinghouse and asked if the station would be interested in running a weekly fashion program. Westinghouse agreed, and Horne's *Fashion Talk*, the first commercial radio broadcast, ran from 7:00 p.m. to 7:15 p.m. one evening a week. At the station's request, Horne's added a weekly *Home Furnishings* program. Both of these programs ran consistently during the 1920s. They were supplemented by other programming, including a 1922 *Radio Beauty Talk*, delivered by Mrs. Gouverneur Morris, whose products were sold in the store and broadcasts during the store's annual Book Fair. During the holidays, KDKA broadcast a program of Christmas carols that the Horne's Chorus presented in the store.

Windows were also important in attracting shoppers. During the 1923 open house for the expanded store, Horne's debuted its annual bridal windows to an audience of thirty to forty thousand people. Using eighteen windows, the store presented themes from the life of its fictional bride, each scene decorated with merchandise available inside. The windows were unveiled by a celebrity.

In 1927, Sophie Tucker raised the curtains on scenes from the bride's life: "The Eyes of Youth," "The Debutant," "Engagement," "Courting," "Boudoir," "Hope Chest," "Wedding Cake," "Presents," "Traveling," "Honeymoon Ship" and "New Home." The scene "First Married Days" included burnt toast on the breakfast table. Figures in the windows were made of wax, and the wax bride wore a white satin gown by Madeleine & Madeleine Paris.

An advertisement for the unveiling reminded shoppers that the "Style Supreme Store" was able to outfit not only the bride, her attendants and family but also wedding guests. A replica of the "Bride's House" could be

Horne's debuted its annual bridal windows with the opening of its upgraded store in 1923. The windows chronicled the bride's life and activities and were wildly popular.

seen on the Sixth Floor. On the Floor of Ideas, thousands of bridal gifts were displayed, including glass and pottery from Lenox, Tiffany, Steuben, Roycroft, Rookwood and Lalique.

In 1927, the crowds at the windows were ten people deep; for those who couldn't see the windows in person, a film was made and shown at the Grand Theater.

Two years later, Pauline Maclean unveiled the bridal windows. While the theme—the bride's life—was familiar, in 1929 the scenes included the "Thrill of an Aeroplane Honeymoon." The windows had taken a year of planning and multiple trips to Europe for props. The bride's bouquet was made in Paris of ostrich plumes and lily of the valley and gardenias carved from white ivory.

The windows received attention outside Pittsburgh as people from across the United States and Europe asked for photos of them. They won numerous awards, including the top prize from the International Association of Display Men.

The bridal windows weren't the only entertainment that Horne's provided to shoppers. During the 1920s, the store continued its annual Doll's Tea

Each bridal window had a theme—here the couple are "Leaving for the Honeymoon." Notice the large car displayed in the background.

The "Bridal Party" window features a bridesmaid and two flower girls. Horne's bridal windows garnered national professional awards for its display staff.

Party, routinely serving thousands of children and their mothers and giving the little girls cups and saucers to take home as favors. The store started an annual Book Fair; in 1926, guest authors included Will James, Grace Livingston Hill, Edgar Guest, Richard Halliburton and Will Durant.

During Fabric Week, a dressmaking cutter was on hand to cut pattern pieces for home sewers who had bought their fabric at Horne's. There was an exhibit of original art in the Horne Picture Galleries and a Dahlia Show with hundreds of blossoms on display and experts speaking on dahlia culture. Of course, tubers were available for sale. In September 1926, shoppers could register for the 4th Annual Cooking School taught by a representative from the Corn Products Refining Company that made cornstarch. She would be using an insulated range hood that would continue to cook food while the range was off. Busy women could leave dinner cooking before leaving for an afternoon of bridge and have a hot meal to serve when they returned.

As a glimpse of things to come, an October 1928 Rayon Exhibit showed the potential of the new synthetic silk. Live models wore fashions from the leading Paris houses, but fashions from American designers were also included. At a time when films were still silent, Horne's displayed, for the first time in Pittsburgh, the DeForest Phonofilm, a talking motion picture where the sound was recorded on the same film as the images.

In October 1928, Horne's celebrated another first. Using the giant dirigible *Graf Zepplin*, the store shipped the first merchandise by air from Europe, including millinery, gloves and handkerchiefs from Paris and jewelry from Berlin. It set a time record for transportation of merchandise from Europe; the store also touted its efficiency in getting the goods through customs and onto the selling floor.

Fashion wasn't the only thing that changed radically during the 1920s. Houses were getting smaller as people spent their money on cars and entertainment. While Horne's continued to advertise "Everything for Outfitting Maids"—it had an entire section of uniforms, aprons, head wear and collars and cuffs for household staff in 1922—fewer of its customers had household help. The annual furniture sale at the store reflected these changes. In January 1927, Horne's had a full-size cottage on display that its staff had furnished and decorated. The store was open in the evening, and a special dinner was served in the tearoom so that husbands and wives could visit the display together. A brochure on the "dream cottage" included furniture prices. The same year, a booklet counseled young people on how to budget for a home, with a list of expenses to consider.

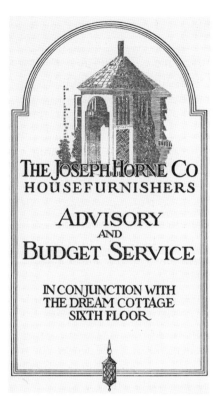

Left: This 1927 promotional card advertises an "Advisory and Budget Service" offered to customers in conjunction with Horne's "Dream Cottage" display.

Below: Horne's Dream Cottage, installed inside the store, represented the smaller new houses that were popular in the 1920s.

Horne's added its first delivery truck in 1903. This later truck was parked in front of the store's warehouse.

Not everyone was choosing to live in a house, no matter how small and efficient. Apartments were becoming fashionable, especially for single people and young couples. Horne's provided decorating services for some of Pittsburgh's newest apartment buildings. An advertisement for the store in 1924 quoted the prospectus for the Morrowfield Apartments on the East End: "The Joseph Horne Co. have complete charge of furnishing the apartments, as well as the foyer, lounge, bridge room, etc., and are enveloping the building in a quiet air of distinctive refinement."

Furniture, of course, would be delivered by the store to "every section of the city, where homes are astir with ambition." To make the deliveries, Horne's continued to expand and upgrade its fleet of trucks. Before Christmas 1923, the store sent twenty-four "of our boys" to Cleveland in a chartered train car to pick up twenty-four three-fourth-ton trucks the store had designed and drive them back to Pittsburgh. They later picked up ten larger trucks. The fleet was further expanded in January 1928 with ten more White trucks—four to deliver packages and six larger trucks for bulk goods.

Again Horne's employees went to Cleveland to drive the trucks back to Pittsburgh. Eight new delivery trucks joined the fleet in December 1929 to help Santa make his rounds. Six were used for out-of-town delivery routes and two for long-distance delivery of furniture.

Horne's also upgraded the downtown store, adding nine new high-speed elevators for passengers and two for freight.

By the end of 1929, Horne's was well positioned as a modern department store. In an advertisement, it proudly related, "Overheard in one of the elevators recently! Two middle-aged ladies, of evident culture and travel, were discussing the store. One, seemingly a visitor, exclaimed in apparent sincere admiration—'This is wonderful! I have never seen a more beautiful store anywhere!' The other, manifestly the hostess, answered: 'Yes, we Pittsburghers are very proud of this store.' 'You may well be,' the visitor continued, 'it is a *truly* metropolitan store.'"

There had been some financial upheavals in the last months of 1929, but economic problems hadn't yet affected the store or its customers. During its eighty years in business, Horne's had weathered multiple economic downturns. Less than ten years earlier, it had continued with plans for expansion in spite of the post–World War I depression. The store's managers had no idea how much their business skills and prudent leadership would be needed in the next decade.

Horne's Weathers the Depression

B y early 1930, it had become clear that the "roaring" economy of the 1920s was just a memory and that hard times were ahead. Not only had the collapsing stock market affected the investment incomes of some of Horne's richest customers, but widespread unemployment also hit the middle class. The purchasing power of the public declined rapidly, and stores had to be creative to stay in business. In spite of their best efforts, many stores closed. Department store sales dropped 41 percent between 1929 and 1933. An article on the upcoming Anniversary Sale in the January/February edition of the *Horne-Pipe*, "The Anniversary Sales Challenge," commented, "This past year has been a hard one for business....Because of the very business conditions, the values of this year's sale are more outstanding than ever."

At least one customer reflected the optimism of the Horne's employees in the *Horne-Pipe* (it's not clear what inspired the customer's note): "Just a reminder of the 'good old days' before America became confused. America's future depends upon the ability of our reliable merchants to weather the storms. I'm sure that Horne's will do it as they always did."

A.H. Burchfield, who had just become store president, responded aggressively to the economic challenges. To attract more business, he moved all of the children's merchandise to the first floor and enlarged the men's department. All of the items for men were consolidated in the larger department, which still had its separate entrance. Mr. Burchfield also enlarged the women's shoe department. One of the largest in the country,

By 1930, Horne's was an established downtown landmark.

it had twenty-four thousand pairs of shoes in stock. Buyer contact with customers was stressed so that buyers would purchase merchandise that customers wanted and could afford. Instead of focusing on sales, staff were encouraged to pursue "superior day-to-day merchandising and service coupled with the best possible values."

A brilliant merchandiser, A.H. Burchfield expanded Horne's women's shoe department during the Depression. The department, one of the largest between New York and Chicago, stocked twenty-four thousand pairs of shoes.

Horne's had also joined the Associated Merchandising Corporation, a consortium of the nineteen largest independent department stores in the country. By pooling their purchasing, the stores could get quantity discounts from manufacturers, which gave them more buying power than the chain stores that were going after their markets. The savings would be passed on to the customers, who would get quality merchandise at economical prices.

By 1930, Horne's was stressing value and economy for those on budgets, realizing perhaps that many of its formerly well-heeled customers were now having to count pennies. On September 30, the store was advertising a line of "Stylethrift" furniture that it had developed, "Horne grade furniture" especially for the "modern small home." In clothing, the term "FashionThrift" was used often for inexpensive but well-designed cotton dresses. By 1932, sales were often dubbed as "thrift events."

On September 1, 1932, Horne's officially opened its downstairs store: "Horne owned, operated, and managed...it specializes in merchandise of approved style, and reliable quality, at definitely established LOWER PRICE levels. Its atmosphere and character are such as to attract discriminating shoppers of limited means." While Horne's had had a sale area in the basement earlier, the downstairs store was much larger and carried its own merchandise, not final sale items from the regular store. In an advertisement, Horne's stated that the new downstairs store was created to attract new customers to Horne's. That may be true since A.H. Burchfield was trying to increase sales, but it was likely that loyal but financially strapped Horne's customers also shopped in the basement.

The store also added lower-priced services. A new Soda Grill with "quick service" and "extremely popular prices" complemented the tearoom. In 1933, the Budget Beauty Shop opened. "Even if you haven't much money, you can still get a lot of attention and beautifying....There's a staff of experienced operators to give you real Horne-type service. And the prices are low enough to let you indulge in frequent visits." A haircut cost just fifty cents and a manicure thirty-five cents.

During the Depression, Horne's added a Soda Grill with fewer frills than the tearoom and lower prices.

As the Depression deepened, local and national governments sought to provide relief. On December 2, 1931, 10 percent of Horne's sales for the day were donated to the Pittsburgh Welfare Emergency Fund. Directors and employees of the store had already donated $37,280 to the fund. The store also supported the National Recovery Act (NRA), which included price controls on merchants. Horne's ads featured the NRA logo, and on September 16, 1933, the store had a float in Pittsburgh's NRA parade. In November, Horne's recognized the Public Works Administration for allocating $135 million to the national railroads for steel rail, steel freight cars and electrical equipment—all Pittsburgh products. "This huge expenditure will mean employment for thousands. Better times are at hand for this section. Face the future with new confidence. Forward Pittsburgh!"

While Horne's recognized the decreased buying power of many of its customers, those with money could still find high-end merchandise. In 1930, the Service Aimcee in Paris, "walking distance from the Ritz and other big hotels," would help Horne's customers with tickets, information and shopping. The infants' wear buyer was traveling to Brussels and Paris for merchandise. A golf pro in the golf shop would give lessons or consult on equipment. The store installed new equipment to clean furs. In April 1931, Horne's advertised new colors for riding habits and smart new uniforms for maids. In March 1932, an advertisement showed cutaway coats for men who wished "correctness and refinement" for Easter.

Ready-to-wear clothing was now accounting for 32 percent of Horne's business. While this included "FashionThrift" clothing and the average ready-to-wear sale was only $7.21, higher-priced clothing was also available: shoppers could pay $125 for a hat, $350 for a dress, $595 for a coat or $6,500 for a fur coat. An advertisement on October 31, 1932, illustrated the disparity in Horne's customers. It announced a fashion show for the new 1932 fur fashions but also advised that the store now had a "Shoe Clinic" where customers could have worn-out or ill-fitting shoes repaired.

By the 1930s, higher duties on imported clothing and decreasing incomes had put Paris fashions out of the reach of most shoppers. Popular fashion now turned to Hollywood for inspiration, and American designers replaced French fashion houses. In a January 31, 1931 advertisement for a "Special Fashion-Thrift Feature," Horne's was selling "California Studio Frocks" and announcing that the Hollywood colony was now setting the fashion. The next year, an advertisement for Chanel sportswear featured costumes designed for Ina Claire, Madge Evans and Joan Blondell in the film *The Greeks Had a Name for Them*. Copies of the costumes were on sale at Horne's. By 1933, similar costume replicas were sold in a dedicated Hollywood Shop. Women could also buy turtleneck sweaters called "Clark Gables" after the actor who had popularized them.

Hollywood did not drive fashion alone. Horne's also hired a Hollywood photographer in 1932 for the store's in-house portrait studio. Two years later, the photographer, Florence Fisher Parry, added two additional Hollywood photographers for the Horne-Parry studio. Horne's also sponsored a series of lectures with Max Factor on "The Magic Art of Make-Up" by Ruth Barton, Max Factor make-up artist in Hollywood.

Celebrity appearances were also popular. In March 1933, the Pennsylvania Railroad's "Movie Star Special" stopped in Pittsburgh on its way to Washington, D.C., for Roosevelt's inauguration. A crowd of fifty thousand people met the train at the station, where the stars—including Tom Mix, Joe E. Brown and Bette Davis—got into cars for a motorcade into town. The first stop was Horne's, where the movie stars made an appearance sponsored by GE.

And there was the celebrity endorsement. A Horne's advertisement featured band leader Fred Waring, a regular Horne's shopper when playing in Pittsburgh. The subject: why he liked to shop in the Men's Store:

> *It pays to buy good things and to deal at good stores....The ability to get what you want when you want it...right prices...related things conveniently grouped together...quick, efficient service...freedom from red tape in handling cash or charge transactions...and a general confidence in the reliability and responsibility of the organization.*
>
> *Mr. Waring mentioned further that he liked the fact that Horne's Men's Store had its own entrance direct from the street, and that a man could satisfy his wants there without running the gauntlet of petticoats, ribbons, thread, powder puffs, and other feminine distractions.*

The trend toward economy did not affect fashion alone. Since the 1920s, houses had been getting smaller, and the economic problems of the 1930s supported the trend. Heavy Victorian furniture would not fit in these smaller homes. An advertisement for a February 1936 sale of "Modern Furniture" was illustrated with smaller pieces of fashionable "modern" Art Deco furniture that customers could buy on a "Budget Plan." An exhibit of Monterey furniture from California included modern designs especially for the "Rumpus Room."

A separate entrance to Horne's Men's Shop allowed men to select merchandise without female distraction.

Horne's also opened a Plan Shop for people who wanted to do their own decorating rather than pay the store for the service. They could buy furniture, fabric and wallpaper in one place and tour a modern four-room apartment. The Plan Shop offered "innumerable ideas for making a small home livable and charming."

Sales of fine china and glass dropped as frugal shoppers focused on necessities, but many of them were tempted by the latest Homer Laughlin product: Fiestaware. As Horne's advertised, "Color everywhere....especially on your table! Have a complete dinner service for eight—50 pieces—for no more than the price of a stereotyped pattern." The cost of the service for eight was a mere $14.95.

By the mid-1930s, the economy had started to improve when Horne's was hit with another disaster. The winter of 1936 was snowy and cold; huge quantities of snow fell across Pennsylvania and didn't melt in the cold temperatures. In March, the weather changed dramatically with warm temperatures and rain. On March 16, a torrential rain across the state sent water to tributaries of the Allegheny and Monongahela Rivers already swollen with snowmelt. The rivers rose, reaching flood stage of twenty-five feet in Pittsburgh by March 17. That night, it rained again, two inches overnight. By March 18, the river water had reached forty-six feet, twenty-one feet above flood stage. Debris from flooded towns and cities upstream coursed through the city in some of the most rapid currents ever recorded. On March 21, the floodwaters finally began to recede.

The city was devastated: 65 percent of the downtown buildings under water, 100,000 buildings destroyed, $250 million in damages, sixty-nine people killed and five hundred injured. Electric power failed on March 17 and was not restored for eight days. The water supply was contaminated, and railroads and trolleys ceased to run. With damage to the steel mills, sixty thousand steelworkers were out of work.

Horne's, located only several blocks from the Allegheny River, had successfully weathered the 1907 Pittsburgh flood. This time, the store wasn't as lucky. The upgraded flood control measures that had been prudently installed were overwhelmed. As the *Pittsburgh Press* reported, "The Joseph Horne Co., at Penn Ave. and Stanwix St., suffered the most, perhaps, because it was closest to the surging Allegheny."

Outside, the floodwater reached almost to the top of the store's marquee and, inside, to the balcony on the first floor. The basement and first floor were completely underwater and all of the merchandise and fixtures destroyed. Insurance didn't cover the damage, but thanks to the prudent managers, Horne's had enough reserves to recover without borrowing any money. As soon as the streets were cleared of debris, employees came to work to start clearing away the damage and cleaning the store. They were paid their full-time wages for every day that they hadn't been able to come to work.

An advertisement on March 26 advised shoppers that Horne's would open soon:

> *Our store is being put into perfect shape for reopening by the best talent money can employ. Under the supervision of Janssen & Cocken, building architects; Mellon-Stuart Company, contractors; C.A. Wheeler, Inc. fixture architects; Raphael Electric Company, electrical contractors; and the Westinghouse Elevator company, assisted by the splendid co-operation of Duquesne Light Company, Equitable Gas Company, and other utilities, as well as city and county authorities and our own resourceful organization.*

The 1936 St. Patrick's Day flood devastated the first floor of Horne's. Floodwaters reached as high as the balcony.

The public was assured that the store would not open until it was safe and sanitary. The river mud had left a foul-smelling mess across the city in the wake of the flood.

With new merchandise and temporary fixtures, the store reopened on April 1, except for the downstairs store and portions of the first floor. The entire first floor was open by April 13, in time for Easter shopping. On the day after the opening, Horne's publicly thanked its customers in an advertisement: "We are deeply moved at the public response to our re-opening yesterday. It was difficult to hold back tears at the outpouring of customers who journeyed here this first day to welcome us back to business....The flood brought us great monetary losses, but it brought us also to a new realization of the grand organization we have and the wonderful, generous, understanding people that make up this world."

On April 3, Horne's installed a large poster in one of the store's windows. "Let us be thankful," it read. "Our losses to building and merchandise were tremendous, but they are nothing compared to that which we would have felt if a single one of our employees had lost his life. From the courage and cooperation of our employees and the loyalty of our friends and customers, out of the flood of 1936 there will emerge A Greater Horne's."

The fixtures that had been installed on Horne's first floor after the flood were just temporary. In 1937, store managers worked to realize "A Greater Horne's," upgrading the flood protection system and installing air conditioning.

The flood protection installed in 1907 was designed to protect the store from a forty-foot flood, but the crest of the historic 1936 flood was forty-six feet. Even though flood control on the Allegheny was planned, store managers decided to protect the store from a forty-eight-foot flood. Designed by Pittsburgh architects Janssen and Cocken and installed by Mellon-Stuart Company, the system was said to be the most elaborate flood protection system in the country.

The sidewalks outside the store were strengthened with waterproof sidewalk vaults, and all non-essential building openings below a twelve-foot water line were sealed with brick and stone. The pumping equipment was upgraded, and an employee flood brigade was organized and trained.

The show windows were equipped with reinforced aluminum bulkheads that would be rolled forward on tracks and bolted in place behind the window glass once the window displays were cleared. They could be lowered and sealed in seven minutes. Additional bulkheads would be brought out of storage and bolted over doorways. The loading dock at the back of the building had bulkheads in the ceiling that would be rolled down.

Inside, the wooden fixtures were replaced with portable steel ones that could be moved to the elevators and taken to upper floors in a future flood. The steel was finished to look like walnut, and the fixtures were trimmed in bronze. With the new fixtures, the merchandise could be cleared from the downstairs store and the first floor in three hours.

In the winter of 1937, Horne's employees had an emergency drill in using the new flood protection system when rising waters in the Allegheny threatened to flood the city. Crowds watched from outside the store as employees lowered the bulkheads over the show windows and bolted them in place.

Upgrading the flood protection system affected the lighting and ventilation in the interior of the store. Ventilation had relied on louvered transoms over the show windows to bring fresh air into the store. Now those louvers were sealed. All of the windows in the first-floor tearoom were also sealed. Horne's managers decided to improve the store's interior air quality.

A.H. Burchfield told the press, "Air conditioning will add comfort and attractiveness to shopping, but will contribute to the health and efficiency of our employees, and will reduce merchandise losses from smoke and dirt, which are a considerable factor in Pittsburgh."

Designed by Dravo-Doyle and installed by Carrier Corporation, it was the largest air conditioning installation in Pittsburgh at the time and cost $450,000. The entire store was air conditioned: the downstairs store and seven upstairs floors, for a total of 7.5 million square feet. Ductwork in the ceilings, concealed with plaster and lath, circulated ninety thousand gallons of water with the cooling power of melting one thousand tons of ice each day. While the system was designed to cool the store, it contributed to more uniform temperatures in the winter as well and saved on steam costs. As it reminded shoppers in its advertising, "Cool Horne's" was the only air-conditioned department store in the city.

One loyal customer visited the updated Horne's to buy a "smart new hat" and a dress. As she shopped, she commented on the "new beauty and

In May 1937, Horne's added air conditioning to improve the interior ventilation of the store and reduce merchandise losses from Pittsburgh's dirty air. Ducts were installed below the original ornate plaster ceiling.

comfort of this store which has been her favorite shopping place for so very many years." She was an excellent judge; at 101, she might have started her Horne's shopping at the Market Street store.

By 1937, the economy had begun to improve and shoppers had more money to spend. While many stores had closed in the challenging business climate in the early 1930s, Horne's had prospered. It now included the air-conditioned downtown store, a parking lot across the street, the nine-story warehouse on the North Side and a four-story warehouse. Horne's also occupied the top two floors of a building next to the store.

In December 1936, it bought twenty-eight new delivery trucks from White Motor Company—nineteen standard trucks, eight oversize furniture trucks and one relay truck for the shuttle service between the store and the service warehouse. "The bodies are the Joseph Horne Co.'s own design, and are of conservative streamlined design finished [in] dark blue with red trimmings." The driver's compartment was completely enclosed and provided with a heater, a window defroster and "similar modern features."

When the new trucks were unveiled to the employees of the delivery department at a meeting, Jerry O'Brian, who had forty-two years of service at Horne's, compared them to the horses and wagons used when he started his career. "The driver was totally unprotected from the elements, and… frost bitten ears and frozen hands were a constant danger in zero weather," he remembered.

The store now had seventy-two delivery trucks, with one assigned to downtown and one to Camp Horne.

Horne's was still holding one store-wide sale per year, the Anniversary Sale in February. It still closed the curtains over the show windows on Saturday night to "respect the Sabbath." The store auditorium was regularly used for cooking schools, fashion shows, home economics lectures, bridge instruction and dressmaking classes. The Personal Services Bureau handled mourning, wedding and travel wardrobes and gift shopping.

Horne's had added a new service for shoppers in October 1931: the Charga-Plate. Those who had a Horne's credit account were automatically sent a Charga-Plate to use. The small metal plate was embossed with the name and address of the holder. There was a card on the back for the owner's signature. When a sale was rung up, the shopper handed the plate to the clerk, who ran it through a machine that printed the embossed information onto the sales slip. While Horne's marketed the Charga-Plate as a convenience to shoppers—no more questions from the clerk or inaccuracy in the slip—it also benefited store bookkeeping. But one new

Challenging economic times didn't mean that people lowered their standards of dress.
Women still bought hats from Horne's millinery department.

clerk who remembered to ask customers for their plates and successfully
ran them through the machine forgot the last part of her training. She
didn't return the Charga-Plates to the customers and had collected seven
plates by her noon break.

During the 1930s, Horne's continued to feature events in the store to draw
shoppers. There were fashion shows, but they were no longer dominated by
designs from leading Paris fashion houses. In May 1934, the store hosted
"The Vogue-Lux Fashion Show…[a] demonstration of how to be your
own summer dressmaker and save money." When many women returned
to home sewing to stretch the family budget, fashion shows sponsored by
pattern companies were regular features in the fabric department.

In 1936, the fashion focus was on women who were now working outside
the home. Using the title "Career Women Do Know Their Fashions,"
Horne's held a clinic for "business and professional women," featuring a
judge, a doctor, business executives, secretaries and teachers. Following the
clinic, there was a "Business Women's Week Fashion Show" in the tearoom

during lunch. The store held a similar event for college girls and "young careerists" several years later.

Store services were also tied to fashion. The Ask Mr. Foster travel service showed a free color movie during a lecture on Bermuda; before the movie, "Fashions for Southern Wear" were modeled in the tearoom during lunch. Horne's also sponsored regular fashion shows for men, including a 1938 Fashion Show and Stag Party at the Pittsburgh Athletic Association and fashion shows for charity, including a June 1939 show of summer fashions for the Social Service Committee of Presbyterian Hospital.

Fashion shows were not the only events held at Horne's. Those seeking free entertainment could find it daily in the department stores. The same week in 1934 as the Vogue-Lux Fashion Show, Horne's was displaying the Ladies' Home Journal Model House Exhibit and the Railway Express Exhibit, both from the Chicago Exposition. There were musical events in the phonograph and piano departments, the annual cooking schools and product demonstrations in the housewares department and bridge classes in the auditorium. A free Baby Development Clinic for mothers and prospective mothers, taught by a trained nurse, included information on planning a baby layette; Horne's certainly hoped that mothers would purchase layette items in its infant department and later children's clothes and toys.

Horne's also continued its radio programming, broadcasting a *Scholastic Sports* program focusing on high school scores and sports news every Friday night from the Floor of Youth. The store also sponsored broadcasts of the Rolling Rock Races from Ligonier on KDKA. Sports fans could come to the store and hear games with commentary by Rossey Roswell.

While Horne's did continue many of its traditions during the Depression, others seem to have fallen by the wayside. There were no more extravagant annual bridal windows after 1929.

The economic challenges of the Depression brought profound changes to the culture that were reflected in the department stores. American designers replaced Parisian fashion houses, and rayon and other synthetic fabrics replaced silk. Houses were smaller, and women doing their own housework were interested in labor-saving appliances like electric toasters, percolators and refrigerators. Women had careers, particularly if they were unmarried and had to support themselves. At the end of the decade, in June 1940, a Horne's advertisement for "California Slack Suits" actually showed women and girls in pants and sailor blouses. A decade earlier, women in Horne's advertisements for golf and tennis clothing were still wearing dresses and skirts for sports.

During the Depression, women were doing more of their own housework, and kitchens were designed to appeal to them. This "Modern Kitchen" features fashionable metal cabinets, stainless steel counters and glass block walls.

By 1939, the country was becoming more optimistic about the economy and its future prospects. This optimism was reflected in the 1939 New York World's Fair. Horne's furnished and decorated the Electric House, one of fifteen model houses in the "Town of Tomorrow," the only decorator outside of New York that participated in the "modern home project." The store also set up a booth in the Consumers Building in the central area of the fair not far from the Trylon and Perisphere. There was nothing for sale in the booth; it was designed to provide travel services and a meeting place for Pittsburghers attending the fair. There were copies of Pittsburgh newspapers and travel information. Those attending the fair could have mail forwarded to the booth and pick it up there. Mr. Burchfield, president of the store, commented, "So many Pittsburghers expect to visit the Fair that we decided to go along ourselves for whatever service we may be. Possibly we can help some find accommodations or through our registry help Pittsburghers locate one another. This service ought to be a pretty good feature of the world of tomorrow."

"Horne's at the World's Fair:" Horne's provided a meeting place for Pittsburghers attending the 1939 New York World's Fair.

While many people were optimistic about the future, others were watching events in Europe and the Far East with alarm. In August 1936, Horne's had recognized the civil war in Spain as nothing more than a fashion opportunity. "Spanish Rebellion Shades a Front-Page Fashion" an advertisement for a dress stated. "This adorable new Junior gown-of-conquest, with the exciting swing of a Spanish tango...in Mediterranean Blue, and Castilian Red...gives you your first taste of the daring new colors that take as prominent a place in the smart world of Fashion, as the Spanish Rebellion holds in world politics!"

Those who were hoping that the next decade would be less challenging would be sorely disappointed.

Horne's Goes to War

By 1940, the United States had recovered from the worst of the Depression, and many people were more optimistic about the future. Their optimism didn't last long. Overseas, years of crises had finally culminated in war. Horne's employee newsletter, the *Horne-Pipe*, noted that men from the Antoine Salon in Paris, parent of the Antoine Salon at Horne's, had been mobilized to fight the invading Germans. Those called up included hairdressers who had visited the salon in Pittsburgh. By June 1941, the *Horne-Pipe* began listing "Boys in Service," and in October, the Horne-Parry photography studio was offering a 15 percent discount on portraits for parents of boys in the service, draftees and enlisted men.

It was not the first time that Horne's had dealt with war. Joseph Horne's trimming business was just starting its second decade when the Civil War broke out. Employees left to join the army, wartime shortages affected what was sold and prices skyrocketed.

War in Europe had already affected the store in 1917. When the fighting started in Europe in August 1914, it had challenged Horne's buyers who had been unable to travel to select merchandise for the store. But until 1917, it was essentially a European war. Americans did join the fighting, but only as volunteers. That changed in 1917, when the United States declared war on the Central Alliance—Germany, Austria-Hungary and Italy—and American soldiers were sent overseas. Among those serving were Durbin Horne's son, Joseph, who was with the infantry in France, and sixty-seven men and women who were represented by stars on Horne's Service Flag.

By June 1917, Horne's was selling made-to-order officer's uniforms for $37.50. In September, shoppers could find regulation army blankets, rubber blankets with eyelets and officer's sleeping bags. For $25, "Friends of the Boys on the Firing Line" could buy an A.E.F. Body Shield used by the British forces in France. The body shield was designed to protect 75 percent of the body's "vital parts" against shrapnel, revolver bullets and bayonets. It could be ordered in Horne's first-floor Soldier Shop or in the Paris Shopping Service department on the sixth floor and would be shipped directly from England to the front lines.

Horne's Soldier Shop had, as it advertised, "many happy answers to the question 'What to Give a Soldier?'" Shoppers could buy prepared gift packets ranging in price from one dollar to ten dollars designed to appeal to those in camp in the United States, or they could select items using the free shopping service.

Horne's Paris Shopping Service, which had earlier served tourists, was now its link to soldiers in France. Friends and family in the United States could send boxes overseas; Horne's regularly advertised suggestions for "the Overseas Box" from the Red Cross. They included toiletries; games, puzzles and playing cards; writing papers, pencils and fountain pens; and slippers and socks. Pocket Kodak cameras were also recommended as gifts for departing soldiers.

Horne's Paris Shopping Service was able to buy and send items that were too heavy to ship from the United States or that wouldn't make the trip. The store reminded shoppers that they could order "Sweaters, Jam, Roast Chicken" that would arrive in time for Christmas if ordered early enough. When later postal regulations made shipping from the United States difficult, Horne's Paris Shopping Service would buy and ship gifts ordered at the Soldier Shop in Pittsburgh.

Patriotic Pittsburghers could do more than just order gifts for soldiers, and Horne's encouraged civilians to do their part. The store was a strong supporter of Liberty Bonds, which the government issued to raise money for national defense. In May 1917, it advertised Liberty Loan Liberty Bonds as a Memorial Day gift. By October, Horne's was advising its customers that the Second Liberty Loan Campaign was beginning and that they could buy bonds at a booth on the first floor. "Fight your Country's Fight with your Dollars. Buy early and often," it exhorted.

On Saturday, October 11, 1918, Horne's participated in a "Liberty Day" program held on a stage in front of the store. The event, presented by the Women's Liberty Loan Committee, included speakers and

In this World War I–era window, Lady Liberty, surrounded by flags of the allied nations, exhorts Pittsburghers to buy war bonds.

entertainment. Inside, singer John McCormack had earlier appeared in the Victrola department, where he autographed a Victor Record of himself singing "The Star-Spangled Banner." He also gave each record buyer a $100 bond.

Horne's employees were also encouraged to buy bonds by a committee of their co-workers. The drive was successful, as the local newspaper reported in April 1918. Employees had bought a total of $180,000 worth of bonds during three bond drives. That total didn't count any of the bonds that had been sold to customers in the store.

Shoppers were encouraged to support the war in other ways. By August 1917, the Council on National Defense had issued suggestions for waste reduction in department stores, including waste labor, and Pittsburgh department stores complied. Shoppers were told not to leave the store empty-handed, but to carry their own purchases instead of having them delivered. "Help to make this 'The Fashion,'" they were asked. They were also asked to bring items to the store that they were returning, buy only what they intended to keep, avoid using COD services and shop in the morning. Stores announced that they would make no more than two deliveries per day to addresses in the city and no more than one per day in the suburbs. They would start to charge for "Special Delivery" services for those who couldn't wait for a regular delivery and to limit and charge for CODs. They instituted a five-day limit on returns. By February 1918, Horne's was also closed on Mondays to conserve heating fuel.

In addition to buying bonds at the Liberty Loan booth or gifts at the Soldier Shop, Horne's shoppers could join the Red Cross at its recruiting station at the West Store Entrance. The station was mobbed with volunteers and those joining the organization for one dollar per year. Women who had signed the conservation pledge of the Food Commission could get patterns for "Hooveralls," the official uniform, for ten cents at the pattern counter. The uniforms, a wraparound apron, were worn as house dresses and "identify the wearer with this great patriotic movement."

Horne's shoppers were also asked to save peach and plum pits and bring them to the store, where a container had been set up on the main floor. The pits would be sent to the government and were used to make gas masks for soldiers. After dropping off their fruit pits, shoppers could stop by the Ribbon Section on the main floor and buy a length of "Allies Ribbon" that combined all of the national colors of "our Entente Allies." The one-and-a-half-inch-wide grosgrain ribbon could be worn as a hat band or fashioned into a badge.

By the spring of 1918, Horne's was once again focusing on French fashion. In an advertisement in May, the store advised customers, "Suits are very much in declares our latest letter from Paris, arrived only this week. The letter continues, 'Every girl in Paris is wearing one, and the houses which turn out smart youthful styles have done a good business in spite of the bombardment.' The war had brought Suits into wider service than ever as the utility garment of a woman's wardrobe. Our stocks are exceptionally large and varied."

An advertisement for the store's three-day fashion opening on September 18 noted the Parisian influence and commented that there would be "more models of this origin than at any Opening in several seasons." It then listed the Paris fashion houses whose work would be presented, with illustrations of the dresses to be modeled.

Two months later, the war was officially over; an armistice had been signed on November 11. "The War Won—Long Deferred Needs for Home and Person May Now Be Taken Up," Horne's announced. "It is a time to be happy, grateful and optimistic! Social activities are being resumed. Plans are being formulated for home-coming receptions, for the returning heroes. Pretty clothes—bright, cheery fashions, which reflect our spirits are again in order. This store sounds the note of new dress in a Silk Sale, befitting the occasion, which starts tomorrow—the largest offering of fine silks, at a single price, in the history of this store." By the following June, Horne's was advertising a service to preserve "your soldier, sailor, or other war-work uniform safe through the years."

The "War to End All Wars" brought peace to Europe for just twenty years. While the United States eventually declared war and sent troops to the front, many Americans were not directly affected in World War I. That changed in World War II. When the Japanese attacked Pearl Harbor and the United States responded, everyone became part of the war economy. Horne's responded much like it had in World War I, but on a larger scale.

Retailing was considered an essential industry during World War II, and department stores and retail trade associations cooperated with the government's command economy. Much of this control was not new; the government had responded to the Depression with economic controls. In April 1941, the Office of Price Administration (OPA) had introduced price controls to fight inflation, but regulations increased with the outbreak of war. The War Production Board was created in January 1942 to allocate critical materials, and rationing was soon driving fashion and determining what consumers could purchase. In January 1942, Pittsburgh's downtown department stores reduced store delivery from daily service to every other day, citing tire rationing and "the necessity of conserving valuable metals for the defense program." Shoppers were asked to carry small packages with them and bring returns to the stores themselves.

Horne's chose the theme "Serving the Hands that Serve the Nation" for its annual Anniversary Sale in February 1942 but didn't list any items on sale. It had been a challenge for the buyers to even find merchandise to include in the sale, and store managers were concerned that limited items would sell out quickly, disappointing customers. Clerks in each department would share information about sales items directly with customers as they shopped. By December 1943, the store advertisement for shoes included directions on which ration stamps to use for the purchase.

Labor shortages also challenged the store. Not only were employees and managers leaving for the military, but finding replacements was also difficult. Stores responded by expanding self-service, which had started decades earlier at sales tables. By November 1943, Horne's was having difficulty getting additional help for the holidays and was asking employees to recruit friends and relatives to work.

Horne's also actively supported the war effort as it had in World War I. By January 1942, it had opened a "Victory Booth" on the street floor to sell defense stamps and war bonds to customers. Employees were

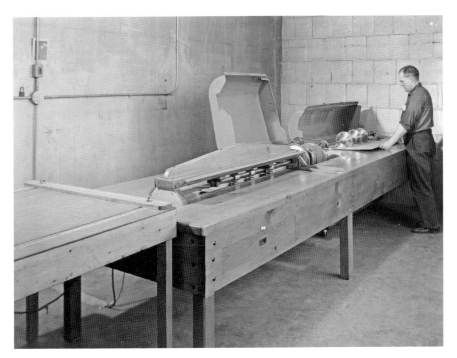

Horne's installed special equipment to recycle cardboard packaging used in the store.
Recycling may have started as a war measure to conserve packaging material.

also encouraged to buy bonds directly from their paychecks. By May 1942, Horne's was the first department store in Pittsburgh to earn a "Minute Man Flag" because 92 percent of the employees had subscribed to the War Bond Payroll Savings Plan. The flag was displayed in the store "to tell Pittsburgh and the world that we're doing our share toward Victory." By November, almost all of the store employees had signed up to buy bonds out of their income.

Horne's also supported bond drives throughout the city. In October 1942, employees participated in the "Women in War" parade, sponsored by the Allegheny County War Bond Committee. In September 1943, Horne's sponsored a Liberty Bond rally at noon on a Tuesday in front of the store's "Liberty Window," where a replica Liberty Bell was on display. The rally featured local celebrities and an appearance of "one of our returned War Heroes." Anyone purchasing a $100 war bond would get a Glenn Miller record autographed by Paula Kelly, who had sung with Glenn Miller's orchestra. In 1944, Horne's installed a teletype machine generating the latest war news in one of its windows for a bond drive.

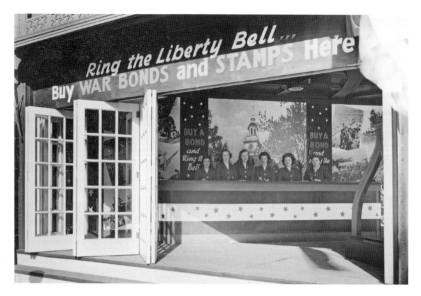

Using a model of the Liberty Bell, Horne's reminded shoppers, "Buy War Bonds and Stamps Here."

In September 1943, Horne's installed a replica Liberty Bell in one of its windows to support a war bond rally held in front of the store. Here "Liberty Girls" pose with the bell.

War bond activities continued throughout the war. By May 1945, anyone buying a war bond in Horne's would receive a ticket for a navy tour of an LST 1059, anchored in the Allegheny River. The ship had been bought with $5 million in war bonds raised in Allegheny County and replaced a ship that had been sunk in the Philippines.

Horne's employees had been joining the service before the war began, but once war was declared, more and more joined up. The "Our Boys in Service" list in the *Horne-Pipe* grew longer and longer. The "First Girl" to become affiliated with the army joined the Recreational Branch of the Red Cross and was soon working at a hospital in Watertown, New York, providing recreation to soldiers in the wards. In February 1942, the first Horne's casualty was recorded, a sailor who had gone missing after the *Jacob Jones* was torpedoed. He had reenlisted after serving in World War I.

In May 1942, a "Horne's Employees in Our Country's Service" tablet was installed on the first floor of the store; a similar service board was hung in the warehouse. One man who had worked in the advertising department was now on the staff of *Yank Magazine*, the store comptroller had left to become the Pennsylvania director of the OPA and a fabrics buyer was on active duty with the Purchasing Division of the U.S. Army. Joseph Horne, grandson of the founder who had served in World War I, reenlisted as a captain. His two cousins who also worked in the store, Joseph G. Horne and Bernard Horne, were serving as naval lieutenants. Horne's training department maintained a list with names and addresses of all of those who were serving, and employees were encouraged to write to them. Soldier news now covered pages and pages of the *Horne-Pipe* as former employees sent letters and photos.

Employees who had not joined up supported their former colleagues who were now at arms. They formed a Nightingale Club to provide soldiers with birthday and holiday gifts. At first, they placed an "Uncle Sam's Hat" in the employee cafeteria to collect spare change, but that soon developed into fundraising events. In the fall of 1942, the club held a dance to raise money for Christmas gifts for those overseas and in the United States. Local soldiers were invited as guests. The Nightingale Club also sent copies of the *Horne-Pipe* to those who were serving; the newsletter received many letters from soldiers thanking the club for the gifts they received.

Employees were busy in other ways too. Employee knitters made 250 garments for the Red Cross, including sweaters, mittens and caps. Someone estimated that it took 138 weeks of steady knitting to produce the clothing. Employees in the Fur Work Room worked evenings to make vests for sailors in the merchant marine.

Joseph Horne Jr., shown here in his World War I uniform, also served in World War II.

Horne's did not merely sacrifice people to the war effort. During the summer of 1942, it was still advertising its store as "Cool Horne's," the only fully air-conditioned store in Pittsburgh. In September, it announced that the War Production Board had requested the two giant compressors from the store's air conditioning system for use in war plants making synthetic rubber and aviation gasoline. The compressors, the only ones in Pittsburgh that the government could use, weighed 100,000 pounds each and could

During World War II, Horne's shoppers could visit a special "Canteen" to find gifts for soldiers.

cool 1,500 gallons of water each minute. Twenty other department stores around the country also turned over their cooling equipment. Horne's assured customers that the store would still use its air conditioning in the summer, cooling the store with water from its wells until the oppressive heat of July and August arrived.

Horne's also encouraged the public to support the war effort. By January 1942, the store was selling Red Cross uniforms, including those worn by canteen staff, for those who were volunteering. The store also offered classes in first aid and, for its employees, defense courses in first aid, home nursing and nutrition. When rationing of canned goods began in early 1943, Horne's developed a "Food Rationing Work Sheet" to help the public budget coupon points. "If you 'spend' all your points at the first of the month," a store advertisement warned, "you may find yourself at the end of the month with a series of skimpy meals." In addition to the worksheet, Horne's provided a Nutrition Center, where volunteer dietetic experts from the government could help customers with their daily menus so that they could get the maximum benefit from their food allotments.

"No ration point worries when you do your own canning," Horne's declared in August 1945, inviting customers to its last Canning Clinic of the summer. During the clinic, Kathryn Barnes, the home services director at Equitable Gas, would demonstrate canning fruits with little or no sugar, as well as the simplest ways to can vegetables. Participants would receive a canning guide, and if they needed equipment or supplies, they could buy galvanized canners, preserving kettles, paraffin and jar rubbers to seal jars, EZ-Seal glass-topped jars and even tin cans in the housewares department.

Horne's also supported the local war effort. On Wednesday, August 26, 1942, Pittsburgh held its first daylight air raid drill. Horne's participated, using the opportunity to test its own Air Raid Precaution (ARP) Program. The store had been designated as an official post by Allegheny County civil defense officials, and store managers had established the ARP program with assigned duties for staff and an operating manual. The plan was also presented in the *Horne-Pipe* so employees would be familiar with the warning signals and would know where to evacuate. "Safety Zones" had been set up on the second, third and fourth floors of the store. "We are confident we can rely upon you to fulfill your obligation in a CALM AND COOL MANNER. Our customers will exhibit as much CALMNESS and CONTROL as we do."

The mock air raid warnings sounded at 1:45 p.m. on Wednesday, when downtown Pittsburgh was crowded with people. At Horne's, clerks closed down their departments and successfully ushered customers to the Safety Zones. Customers and employees in the beauty salon, tearoom and the fitting rooms weren't required to evacuate. The *Horne-Pipe* declared the drill a success—everyone must have remained CALM AND COOL.

In spite of the war, Horne's carried out much of its business as usual. In keeping with its reputation for fashion, the store advertised nationally in *Vogue, Town and Country, Harper's Bazaar, Junior Bazaar* and *Charm*. There was a College Shop for those in school; *Vogue*'s College Wardrobe was only available in Pittsburgh at Horne's, and the store advertised in *Mademoiselle*'s college issue. Teenagers were recognized as important customers, too, with their own high school advisory board.

Antoine was still making appearances in his namesake salon, and events across the store provided entertainment for shoppers: a Peruvian Exposition, glass blowers from Corning demonstrating how the company made Pyrex glassware, Chippewa basket weavers and an ice carver.

In the middle of the war, Horne's got the opportunity to test the flood protection system it had installed following the devastating 1936 flood. The Allegheny River hit its thirty-four-foot flood stage at 3:00 p.m. on

During World War II, Horne's continued its focus on fashion in spite of wartime restrictions, running advertisements in New York fashion magazines like *Vogue* and *Harper's Bazaar*.

January 8, 1943, and all of Horne's customers and non-essential female employees were asked to leave the store. (The women at the switchboard stayed.) At 5:15 p.m., men began to move the fixtures and merchandise from the downstairs store; it took them less than two hours. While the water outside rose ten inches above the sidewalk, the only water to enter the store seeped through the pavement and dripped down the walls of the downstairs store. It was easily mopped up. Many employees stayed all night to operate

In January 1943, Horne's got the opportunity to test its upgraded flood protection system as floodwaters surged in front of the store. The system worked, and the store wasn't damaged.

the flood protection system, while the cafeteria served dinner, coffee and snacks. By 8:30 p.m., the water was receding from its 36.6 maximum with no damage to the store. Horne's employees who had to leave used a ladder from the balcony window to reach boats moored in front of the store.

Employees at the warehouse fought the flood too. Everything was moved from the basement and the first floor, bulkheads were put in place and all of the delivery trucks were taken to the upper floors, where they were parked bumper to bumper in the halls. The warehouse cook stayed all night with the other employees making sandwiches and coffee.

By 1945, the end of the war was in sight. Horne's rushed window displays to mark V-E and V-J Days and provided a tribute in its windows to Roosevelt when he died suddenly. At Navy Day on October 27, Horne's celebrated as four ships—an LCS6, LSM-R and two PT boats—docked on the Allegheny at Stanwix Street. While the PT boats made runs back and forth in the river, a Naval Air Torpedo Squadron flew overhead.

At the end of World War II, Horne's displayed models of postwar suburban housing.

With the war in Europe over by August, Horne's advertised that it was again "completely air conditioned"; the compressors had been returned to the store. Horne's employees in the service also began to return to the store. By November 19, veterans were back, and by December, only 223 former employees were serving in the military—9 would never return. The first casualty was a popular young man who had joined Horne's in 1937 and was killed in Cebu, Philippines, while serving in the U.S. Army Air Force. The eight others included men killed in the infantry in Germany, a fighter pilot who died in Europe, a POW who died in a camp in Germany and a soldier who was killed in the Solomon Islands.

Those who returned and the civilians at home were looking forward to a return to normalcy after the war. Horne's, like retailers across the country, recognized those dreams and encouraged them. A 1945 store exhibit featured miniature models of six Post War Homes: a City Home, Suburban Home, Farm Home, Workers Home, Summer Home and a Home for Two.

Celebrating One Hundred Years

By 1946, World War II wasn't forgotten—Horne's participated in a clothing drive for war-torn areas in January—but the defeat of the Axis ushered in an era of optimism. Not only were consumers eager to buy all of the things that had been unavailable during the war, but the technologies and materials developed for the military could also be adapted for the public. People were hungry for all things "modern"—plastics, synthetic fabrics, electrical appliances and more.

To modernize its store, Horne's installed escalators in January 1947; installation costs of the "Electric Stairways" were almost $1 million. The store also installed a complete dial telephone system and modernized many of its departments.

As one historian commented, consumers were eager to "feather their nests" for the postwar baby boom. Furniture sales soared, and stores expanded their furniture departments. Housing sales took off, especially in the suburbs, where developers built hundreds of tract houses. Horne's regularly featured model houses in its store and cooperated with builders in furnishing and publicizing model homes.

Young couples were filling their houses with furniture, but Horne's also sold all of the trappings of modern housekeeping—rugs, curtains, linens, glass, china and cleaning supplies. A small booklet from 1948, titled "Horne's October News," looks like a catalogue from the housewares department. There are pages and pages of small electrical appliances. One entire spread was devoted to Westinghouse appliances, including irons, electric percolators, toasters and the iconic Westinghouse Roaster Oven.

Horne's installed escalators in its downtown store in January 1947. On the left, the housewares department is full of merchandise for buyers eager to feather their postwar nests.

The headline proclaimed, "Pittsburgh's Pride....Westinghouse the Name that Quality Built."

In many ways, Horne's returned to business as usual. There were regular sales without restrictions on the goods that could be offered. Fashion was no longer driven by rationing requirements. It was possible again to get merchandise from overseas.

Horne's had a long relationship with Pittsburgh-based Westinghouse and featured its iconic mixers and roasters in the store for postwar shoppers eager to buy the latest electrical appliances.

Horne's continued to entertain its customers to get them into the store. It held annual spring flower shows. Duncan Hines appeared in the book department to autograph his books on dining. When the national "Freedom Train" visited Pittsburgh in September 1948, the store encouraged customers to attend and distributed information in the store. Horne's held an Aluminum Living Show with a Technicolor film featuring Alan Ladd describing the discovery of the metal. Everything in the show was made of aluminum, including a small airplane that was brought into the store through a sixth-floor window. The wings and tail had been removed so that it would fit and then reattached for the exhibit.

In 1947, Horne's co-sponsored the Pittsburgh Opera Society's performances of Engelbert Humperdinck's opera *Hansel and Gretel*. There were merchandise tie-ins and displays throughout the store, and the event was featured on tearoom menus. Half of the ticket receipts for the event were donated to charity.

Fashion shows were also regular events. Paris fashion was back with the advent of the "New Look"—full, mid-calf skirts and cinched waists. In addition to the regular fashion shows in the store, Horne's provided fashion shows for community organizations like women's clubs and for charity functions. In 1947, the store worked closely with the Pittsburgh Athletic Association on a show, "Gunning for Spring," based on the Broadway show *Annie Get Your Gun*. The show featured American designers in high-end vignettes: airline flight, horse racing, golf, skiing, travel to tropical resorts and California ranches. People in the audience dressed up for the event, which was followed by dancing. In 1948, Horne's helped the PAA develop a Gay Nineties Fashion Show; the invitation was an artificial paper moustache that could be detached and worn at the show.

In addition to advertising, show windows tempted people to come into department stores and shop. Horne's had an outstanding display department that won multiple national awards for its windows. In December 1948, the corner window on Stanwix Street featured a display from Paris. There, the shops of St. Honore had done a series of windows on the theme "Seven Capital Sins." The sin of Idleness featured in Horne's window

After World War II, Horne's continued to organize fashion shows for community groups, including The Fashion Handicap at the Pittsburgh Athletic Association.

was represented by Sleeping Beauty, who reclined surrounded by priceless miniature French antiques. The window was sponsored by Lucien LeLong fragrances and had only been seen in New York.

Perhaps the most famous person to work on Horne's windows was Andy Warhol (then Andy Warhola), who was a part-time employee in the display department as a Carnegie Tech student in the summer of 1947. Longtime Horne's employees remembered that the artist wore such ragged clothes that some of them asked their wives to assemble pants, shirts and shoes to give to him. While he was grateful for the clothing, he cut the sleeves off the shirts and painted the shoes silver before wearing them to work.

A single piece remains from Andy Warhol's days at Horne's. He had painted a floral still life on a piece of drywall for a window and liked it so much that he cut the art out of the drywall and kept it. It has occasionally been on exhibit at the Warhol Museum.

Horne's expanded its services after World War II, adding the Gun Repair Shop in the spring of 1948. "War souvenir guns can be put into prime condition." Geared to hunters, the shop complemented the department that sold fishing equipment and supplies. Horne's also opened the Party Shop where party planners would provide party ideas, games, favors and even cakes for children's parties.

Potential customer markets expanded as well. Horne's had recognized the college market by the late nineteenth century, advertising its expertise in outfitting students headed for eastern schools and colleges. When college enrollment exploded after the war, Horne's responded with seasonal annual College Shops for men and women. The store also started a College Advisory Center, a forerunner of later store College Boards. The ten advisors were all white, and most of them attended either local schools or well-known eastern colleges. Horne's held a college tea for students in late August with a show of college fashions and advised that girls going off to school make their travel arrangements through the store. They offered to arrange for personal shoppers who would shop for students year-round and send merchandise to them at school.

To help students plan wardrobes for college life, Horne's provided lists of items for a "Basic Wardrobe"; the lists, divided by gender, ran for several pages. In 1948, the basic wardrobe for men included multiple coats and raincoats, a minimum of two suits, slacks and sports jackets and a minimum of six white shirts. That wasn't all—the list recommended that men have additional colored sports shirts, hats, tails and a tuxedo for evening wear with appropriate accessories, as well as sports clothing for tennis, golf, riding and skiing. There was a list of dorm items—linens, radio, lamps—and the luggage to carry it all.

The 1947 "Basic College Wardrobe for Girls" was no less extensive. The list suggested several casual coats and raincoats plus a dress coat that could be either cloth or fur—muskrat, beaver and opossum were popular. Girls, like the boys, should pack several suits, including a "little black suit," blazers and four or five shirtwaist dresses. "It is necessary to have a white dress at most schools," the list noted, as well as several date dresses. "Pretty crepes for faculty teas and little evenings...at least one sophisticated black dress." That wasn't all: three or four skirts, lots of different blouses and eight to ten sweaters were included—"Cashmeres to be worn inside the skirt."

For evening, there were more dresses: "off shoulder necklines, and one strap styles rate high" and evening wraps, "generally fur coats." Although girls did not wear pants to class, the list suggested gray flannel shorts for winter and "pedal pushers" and advised that "blue jeans are No. 1." The list concluded with multiple bras, girdles and slips, as well as an entire page of

Horne's embraced the new technology of television, broadcasting from the store in 1949. It developed a close relationship with WDTV, later KDKA.

accessories—gloves, stockings, scarves, handkerchiefs, hats, shoes, handbags and linens. A wardrobe trunk, wardrobe suitcases and hat and shoe boxes were recommended to carry all of the necessary clothing.

After World War I, Horne's had been instrumental in introducing radio, a technology developed during the war, to Pittsburgh. Now, after World War II, the new technology was television. In September 1948, Horne's opened a Television Salon in its radio department and began to advise customers about the technology, explaining, "Before any television set is installed in a home or commercial establishment, a telecast station should be in operation transmitting a test pattern." A radio set could be used to pick up transmissions but only to provide sound to a TV. The store had "many Television instruments" on display, not yet for sale but designed to show customers how a television set could supplement radio for home entertainment.

Pittsburgh got its first television station when WDTV went on the air on January 11, 1949; Horne's sponsored the first public service television program, *A Salute to Pittsburgh*, which aired at 6:30 p.m. the next day. Pittsburgh leaders watched the program on a tiny screen in the Duquesne Club, and the public could watch on sets in Horne's television department.

Television programming became a regular Horne's marketing strategy, as well as a way to support the pioneering WDTV station (W DuMont Television), which was owned and operated by DuMont at the time. It provided the first "network" by connecting stations in different cities via coaxial cable. Westinghouse bought the station in 1954 and renamed it KDKA. Horne's first broadcast developed into a regular news feature that appeared from 6:30 p.m. to 6:45 p.m. on Mondays, Wednesdays and Fridays.

Soon Horne's was selling radio/television combinations for home entertainment. By the summer of 1949, the store was regularly inviting the public to watch special broadcasts in its Assembly Hall. Baseball was featured on July 12, when fifteen large-screen DuMont TVs were set up in the air-conditioned hall and three thousand people came to watch the All-Star Game. It was the first All-Star Game to be telecast in Pittsburgh. Horne's repeated the event in October 1949 for the World Series.

The only real challenge Horne's faced in the years following World War II was a citywide power strike in the fall of 1946. On September 24, all department stores in Pittsburgh were forced to close when power was shut off. Horne's was able to reopen with limited services on October 7, but the power allotted to the store by Duquesne Light wasn't enough to run the store. Horne's managers brought in three diesel generators for supplemental power,

Horne's invited the public to watch the All-Star baseball game, telecast in the cool comfort of its television salon.

but they weren't enough, so the store bought two more. The generators were delivered so quickly that the factory didn't have time to paint them.

The generators provided enough power for light but not enough to run all of the elevators, so most of the employee elevators were turned off; two were left working. There wasn't enough steam for hot water, so the beauty salon wasn't able to provide shampooing; the only service it was able to offer were manicures. The alteration department, which relied on heavy steam presses, was using small, old-fashioned steam boilers to provide steam to the machines. The tearoom was serving a limited menu by candlelight, and the cafeteria could serve only sandwiches, ice cream, coffee and milk for employees. As compensation, coffee and milk were free during the emergency. To provide heat for the store, a locomotive was brought to the elevated tracks on Duquesne Way and lines run from it into the building.

The greatest impact of the strike was on public transportation. No trolleys or buses were operating, so employees were encouraged to carpool. Horne's was able to set up an auxiliary parking lot for six hundred cars on

During an electricity strike, Horne's managers arranged to have a locomotive park on nearby rail lines to provide heat for the store.

the North Side close to the store's service warehouse with the help of the Baltimore and Ohio Railroad, which owned the property. Three station wagons operated as shuttles from the lot to the store, leaving every ten minutes. The lot was also available for shoppers, who could park there and take a shuttle to the store. Horne's advertised it as safe, with full-time attendants and a rainproof shelter.

During the strike, Horne's was opened for limited hours from 9:30 a.m. until 4:30 p.m. Limited bus and trolley service returned on October 14, and normal store hours returned when the strike was over.

By the end of the decade, Horne's was looking forward to a major milestone in its history: the store's centennial in 1949. It had begun preparing for the big event one year earlier by completely refurbishing the entire store. After the 1936 flood, the receiving department had been moved from the basement to the Assembly Hall, which limited the events that could be held in the store. Horne's extended the eighth floor, moved the receiving department there and reopened the Assembly Hall. New murals were painted for the tearoom.

Women's fashion was moved to the fourth floor, where the Fashion Galleries were built, the "new home for many of America's greatest designers of fine clothes." Crystal chandeliers hung from the ceiling, and there were antique mirrors on the walls. The furniture was Louis XV and French Provincial and the carpeting rose beige with rose and green accents. The space was designed to showcase French and American designers: Adrian, Irene, Dior, Hattie Carnegie, Pattulo, Ben Reigs, Joseph Halpert, Davidow, Herbert Sandheim, Fox-Browne, Milgrim, Anna Miller, Adele Simpson and Ceil Chapman. The Fashion Galleries were conveniently located next to millinery; the area also included jewelry, scarves and bags to accessorize the clothing.

Horne's had developed a centennial logo, which was used throughout the entire store and on the awnings outside, as well as on the Jenkin's Arcade sign, which had been illuminated in the 1930s. Delivery trucks were upgraded and painted with the logo. It appeared on centennial flags and printed items: a "Customer Calendar"; "History of the Store"; "Booklet of

Following World War II, Horne's added an additional floor to the top of the store. In this construction photo, the old roof garden is being demolished. In the early twentieth century, the space next to it had been used as a bicycle school.

Centennial Editorials," which had appeared in the local press; menu covers; monthly statements to customers; store posters; and postcards. Shipping labels, letterhead, boxes and shopping bags and store uniforms all featured the centennial logo.

To commemorate the occasion, Horne's also commissioned a centennial fabric designed by Skinner and Bianchini that was sold in the fabric department. The rayon prints came in a full range of colors. "Subtly included in the designs are smoke stacks, bridges, the Golden Triangle, mountain laurel, the sky line, blast furnaces, and landmarks." Two floral prints from 1849 were also reproduced.

Horne's also commissioned a Centennial Plate designed by store staff and made locally by Shenango Pottery. Blue and white, it featured an 1849 scene of the Point in the center and illustrations of historic Pittsburgh industries around the rim. There was also a centennial milk glass plate made by Westmoreland Glass, a souvenir jug, paperweights embedded with antique coins and ash trays and highball glasses with the logo for special guests.

Horne's launched its centennial celebration on February 21, 1949. The store was closed until noon so that employees could celebrate a centennial breakfast. The press, including members of the retail trade press from New York, were also invited, as were the heads of sixty other century-old firms. Three grandsons of the original founders—A.H. Burchfield, store president; Bernard S. Horne, general superintendent; and Joseph G. Horne, department manager—greeted the guests. The employees presented President Burchfield with a bronze plaque commemorating the occasion.

The breakfast featured one of several giant birthday cakes prepared for the centennial kickoff. There were one hundred candles on the cake—ninety-nine plain candles and one centennial candle. A.H. Burchfield lit the candles; they were blown out by the oldest member of the Fifty Year Club at the breakfast. (Sixteen members of the club attended; seven were still working at the store.)

Three giant birthday cakes had also been prepared for the press. Like the cake at the store, they were five tiers high, thirty inches tall and thirty-six inches wide. Only the bottom tier was real cake, designed to serve one hundred people; the other four tiers were decorated cardboard. Still, the cakes were heavy and awkward. Horne's employees used a truck to deliver them to the editors of three leading Pittsburgh newspapers: the *Post-Gazette*, the *Pittsburgh Press* and the *Pittsburgh Sun-Telegraph*. Two employees rode in the back of the truck to safeguard the cakes; two others were instructed to walk each cake through the press offices so that reporters could see them arrive.

At the employee breakfast celebrating Horne's centennial in 1949, the oldest member of the Fifty Year Club cut the Centennial Birthday Cake.

Horne's opened to the public at noon. Outside, the store windows were a "Salute to the Forces that Have Made Pittsburgh Great"—oil, coal, steel, aluminum, electrical goods, glass, transportation and communication, food, labor and science/education. Inside, the store was decorated with flowers, and "Belles of 1849" dressed in historic costumes copied from *Godey's Ladies Book* greeted shoppers. On the "electrical stairways," vignettes showed "old time scenes": "The Family Sits for a Photograph," "The Family Sings on a Sunday Evening," "The Family Goes on a Buggy Ride," "The Family Goes Walking in the Park," "Waiting at the Station for a Train," "Father Misses the Train," "Mama Gets the Dinner," "Mama and Sister Do the Dishes" and "Mama Dusts the Parlor."

Later that evening, Horne's held a centennial dinner for local industrialists and business leaders and an hourlong *Gala Radio Program* was broadcast over KDKA.

The opening kicked off a year of store celebrations, including a full calendar of fashion shows. There was a Centennial Fashion Show presented in the store on February 22–23, with guest speaker Mildred Morton, executive editor of *Vogue*. Under the direction of Fashion Director Edith Shaw Stewart, the show featured fashions by Dior, Milgrim, Adrian, Adele Simpson, Pattulo and Irene of California. It was followed by a Soda Set fashion show for high school students on February 26, in conjunction with *Seventeen* magazine and with Patti Page as a guest. On March 30, there was a Centennial Fashion Show for the Bride.

In August, a College Fashion Show was followed by a show of Foundations for Fall Fashions, with the theme "Fashion Begins in the Corset Department." Presented in conjunction with Warners, the show featured bras, girdles and corsellettes, as well as junior girdles and bras. Another Soda Set Roundup presented fall fashions for teens and the Famous Designers Show noted fall fashions for their mothers. There was also a Business Girls fashion show with pilot Jacqueline Cochran as a guest, an Accessories Show, a Children's Fashion Show and a Fashion

Displays throughout the store focused on change during Horne's one hundred years in business, including this display of bathing suit fashion.

Show of Fabrics and Patterns from *Vogue* Patterns. Horne's presented traveling centennial fashion shows around the region, as well as a televised fashion show.

Fashion shows were not the only events. In May, Horne's sponsored the Centennial Show of Pittsburgh's Industrial Leadership it its Assembly Hall. The industrial leadership theme was featured on menus in the tearoom and in editorials in the local press. "Family nights" in the store were held for families of those who worked in local industries.

Horne's had sponsored an annual Book Fair in the store's book department, but in 1949, it pulled out all of the stops for the October event. Forty-three authors and illustrators were on hand throughout the week to autograph books, and an article on the event appeared in *Publisher's Weekly*, a New York trade journal. Horne's had arranged for the local press to review many of the books.

Adult authors included Dr. Norman Vincent Peale, Margaret Bourke-White, Rex Stout, Paul de Kruif, Will Rogers Jr., Bennett Cerf, Walter Farley, Gladys Tabor and Earnestine Gilbreth-Carey, who wrote *Cheaper by the Dozen*. On Children's Day, authors included Munro Leaf, local writer Marie McSwigan, Marguerite de Angeli and Marguerite Henry, winner of the 1949 Newberry Medal for *King of the Wind*. Exhibits of rare book binding, Braille books and "Books of the Past Century," best sellers since 1849, were on display, and pictures of the featured authors were in Horne's corner window.

The Book Fair wasn't the only major event. *Better Homes and Gardens* magazine selected Horne's to build and design the rooms for a cover article on use of plastics in modern living. A model of the "Plastic House" was on display in the store with copies of the original article, and the home furnishings editor compared nineteenth-century and modern housekeeping during a tour. The Plastic House reduced housework, the presentation claimed, "with plastic coverings in your home, you don't have to scold and nag." The Plastic House didn't just have plastic covers on the couch—there was DuPont nylon carpeting, synthetic fabrics, artificial plastic leather and plastic wallpaper.

For the centennial, Horne's planned a full schedule of events. In May, there was a Tulip Show, followed by Girl Scout and Boy Scout open houses, where scouts demonstrated their skills, and a Sportsman's Fair, where 150 guns owned by the Horne's gunsmith were on display. The store held its annual Doll's Tea, but now the event was open to both girls and boys.

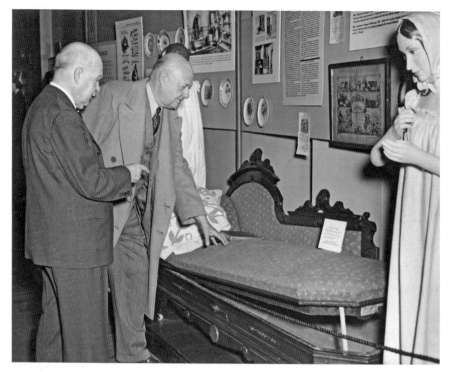

Horne's store managers examine a nineteenth-century metal bathtub concealed inside a chaise lounge during a tour of centennial displays.

Centennial contests and competitions were big events too. Horne's sponsored competitions in high school fashion, college fashion, fabric design, sewing and architectural design. There was a fly-casting tournament and a contest to guess how many smaller candles could be made from a giant birthday candle. A high school centennial square dance contest was won by a team from Wilkinsburg High School; all of the boys competing received a centennial key chain, and the girls were given bottles of Jodelle perfume.

At the end of 1949, Horne's was a major power in Pittsburgh's retail scene. It was still the only fully air-conditioned department store in the city. Its eight-story downtown store provided customers with 160 selling departments on sixteen acres of floor space. Downstairs were 31 departments across thirty-five thousand square feet of selling space targeting customers with annual incomes of $2,500 to $4,000. The store claimed that the wrapping tissue it ordered each year would reach from Pittsburgh to Mexico City and that the blue twine would reach to London.

For shoppers who couldn't come into the city, forty people were available to take orders over the phone.

Electric stairways, installed in 1948 and 1949 at a cost of almost $1 million, could carry 8,000 people per hour. The Assembly Hall could seat 1,000 people and the tearoom 350. There were 547 telephones in the store on 93 trunk lines and 40 people taking telephone orders. Horne's employed about 4,000 people, with 5,500 people working during peak seasons; 291 of those had been with the store for twenty-five years and 16 for fifty years. The employee cafeteria served three thousand meals each day.

In addition to the main store, Horne's occupied a four-story annex next door and operated the Service Building and Warehouse on the North Side that included a basement and eight floors, each covering forty-five thousand square feet, as well as four smaller warehouses.

Like many other downtown department stores, Horne's had also made its first foray into the new suburbs, opening a South Hills store in 1945. It was small at first, only 9,000 square feet, and carried only women's and children's clothing. But business was so brisk that Horne's expanded the store by 4,500 square feet in the fall of 1949.

As customers, employees and local leaders lauded Horne's during its centennial year, they extolled the business acumen of its founders and their descendants, predicting confidently that the store would be around for another one hundred years. Little did they realize that Horne's small foray into suburbia would herald a change in retail that would consume the downtown department store.

Horne's Moves to Suburbia

When Horne's opened its first branch store in Mount Lebanon in 1945, it may have seemed like nothing more than a convenience for South Hills shoppers. But the model houses that the store displayed and decorated were not built in city neighborhoods. The 1953 and 1955 *Better Homes and Gardens* Five Star Houses, for example, were built in Mount Lebanon, one of the area's fastest-growing suburbs. Horne's shoppers could get plans for the houses at the store to build in the suburbs.

The flight of city dwellers to the suburbs, coupled with urban renewal and the destruction of city neighborhoods, would bring profound changes to the country and to downtown retail. That change wasn't readily apparent during the 1950s and 1960s. Horne's business continued as it had, as the flagship store was supplemented by its suburban branches.

After World War II, the car changed everything. The federal government funded highway construction; highways made it easy to live outside the city and commute to work. Between 1950 and 1955, the country's suburban population grew seven times faster than the city population. While downtown stores were concerned about parking, they didn't generally support mass transit from the suburbs that would allow shoppers to get into town. Retail financing also favored the development of suburban shopping malls where shoppers could park for free. While many department stores sited their suburban branches in malls, malls favored chain stores like Penney's, providing more competition.

Urban renewal also affected downtown stores. Tax policies favored new construction over restoration of existing buildings, and older city neighborhoods were often seen as blighted. In Pittsburgh, urban renewal focused on the lower Hill District and parts of the North Side, as well as at the Point. While Horne's managers were actively involved in the Allegheny Conference, which drove the city's urban development, they seemed most focused on the Point, where the Allegheny and Monongahela Rivers converged to form the Ohio. Plans for the Point included a park and a cluster of office buildings called Gateway Center.

When the agreements to begin work at the Point were signed on February 14, 1950, Horne's celebrated with a party in the store's Assembly Hall, complete with Valentine's Day refreshments. Almost four years later, in October 1953, at least one of the Gateway Center buildings was ready for tenants, and Horne's moved its Piano and Organ Salon across the street in time for the Steinway centennial. Store employees rolled pianos across Stanwix Street to their new location.

Urban renewal at the Point included development of office buildings at Gateway Center. Here existing buildings across from Horne's on Stanwix Street are being demolished.

Merchandise for a suburban lifestyle could be bought in downtown stores. Here a model demonstrates a portable Coleman Folding Camp Stove in Horne's sports department.

The country's embrace of the suburban lifestyle was apparent even in the downtown department stores. More and more advertisements featured sportswear, as well as swing sets and sandboxes for the children of the baby boom. In May 1950, "Charcoal Charlie," the "king of outdoor chefs," visited Horne's to demonstrate grills and outdoor cooking methods. As late as 1964, Horne's was selling lawn and garden supplies, as well as lawn mowers.

When downtown department stores built branches in suburbia, they saw those stores as an extension of the main store downtown. They thought that branches would strengthen the downtown stores. Since suburban stores didn't carry the breadth of merchandise that was available downtown, many shoppers did travel into the city. The most faithful downtown shoppers during the 1950s, for example, were suburban women interested in fashion. But the branch stores catered to a single group—white, middle-class shoppers—and provided a safe, controlled atmosphere for them. Many shoppers saw no need to go to the downtown store.

Horne's first branch store in Mount Lebanon was a modest affair. Opened to the public on May 9, 1945, on Washington Road, it originally included only women's and girl's clothing. Before the formal opening to the public, Horne's held a preview with a special lunch for women on the boards of local women's clubs. The store ordered three thousand pots of ivy as favors for the guests. Invitations for an evening preview on May 8 were mailed to twelve thousand South Hills residents. The store was so popular that it opened a Boy's Shop on August 25, 1945. Three Pirates players—Frank Gustine, Jim Russell and Lee Handley—were there to greet shoppers, and Horne's held a drawing for an autographed baseball. Between 1949 and 1959, the Mount Lebanon branch was enlarged and a Home Store was added.

Horne's Mount Lebanon branch was so successful that the store added a second branch in Brentwood/Whitehall in 1951 at Whitehall Terrace. A portion of the store was open in time for Christmas, and shoppers could find cosmetics, accessories, Christmas cards and men's furnishings. Santa presided over the Toy Store. Like the Mount Lebanon branch, Brentwood/ Whitehall expanded over the years, adding a Budget Store in August 1961 and an Auto Center in May 1962.

Horne's third branch opened in May 1953 at the newly built Pittsburgh International Airport. The store, called Horne's Fads n Frills, was located on the main rotunda and carried mostly accessories, including stockings, purses and fashion jewelry, as well as stationery, gifts and toys. A chartreuse frill decorated the windows, and French-style line drawings inside depicted the downtown store and the store branches in Mount Lebanon and Brentwood/ Whitehall. Fixtures were silver-gray oak.

To deliver merchandise from the main store to the new airport store, Horne's used a helicopter. At 9:30 a.m. on May 30, the helicopter landed on the roof of the Stanwix Parking Garage, where the merchandise was loaded; the public was invited to watch from Horne's seventh floor and from Gateway 2. The store used the occasion for media coverage, announcing that it was the first time merchandise was transported from a main store to a branch by helicopter.

Horne's fourth branch, Natrona Heights, opened in a forty-seven-acre shopping mall northeast of Pittsburgh in 1956. It covered sixty-five thousand square feet on a single floor and was designed to serve the employees of Allegheny Ludlum, PPG and Alcoa who lived in the area.

Horne's next branch was closer to home, a gift shop in the nearby Hilton Hotel's lobby. The Hilton Galleries Shop carried gifts and accessories,

Horne's opened a small branch called Fads n Frills at the new Pittsburgh International Airport.

mainly for women, and was designed for men who wanted to buy a quick gift without having to come into the store.

Horne's opened its sixth branch back in suburbia in 1960. As an anchor of the East Hills Shopping Center, the store covered 148,000 square feet, with 40,000 square feet of retail space. It was constructed of white glazed brick and sandstone and accented with blue faience mosaic tile. Outside there were planters on three sides of the store and a garden on the fourth side; the green sidewalks were heated to melt snow in the winter. Inside, Westinghouse Electric Stairways and a Westinghouse elevator carried shoppers between the two floors, and the entire store was air conditioned. In 1961, a budget store was opened in a separate building at Horne's East Hills location.

Horne's seventh branch store, opened in 1962, was also in a shopping mall, Northway, at McKnight Road and Babcock Boulevard in the North Hills. Northway, built on a twenty-nine-acre site, was touted as one of the area's first fully enclosed shopping malls. Shoppers could park outside—the

Merchandise for the new airport store was delivered by a helicopter, which departed from the top of a Gateway Center building.

parking lot held eight thousand cars—and once inside go from store to store in a climate-controlled atmosphere. The two-level mall with escalators and elevators was designed to function like a traditional town square and was landscaped with tropical plants and trees. There were pools and fountains and aviaries with rare birds. Horne's advertisements called it "the tropical mall where it's always spring." The Horne's store covered 160,000 square feet on two levels and included a Budget Store and an outdoor garden shop. It was constructed of white glazed brick, fieldstone and blue vitrineer tile. Inside, a 60-foot clear span between columns allowed for easier shopping, and custom flooring was used to designate different departments.

Unlike its competitor, Kaufmann's, whose free-standing branch store had been built across McKnight Road, Horne's did not include a tearoom. Restaurants in the center of the mall provided lunch and dinner for shoppers.

Horne's constructed two more branch stores in the suburbs in 1965, both of them in shopping malls. The first, officially opened at 9:45 a.m. on March 8, 1965, was in Greengate Mall outside Greensburg. It was designed as a

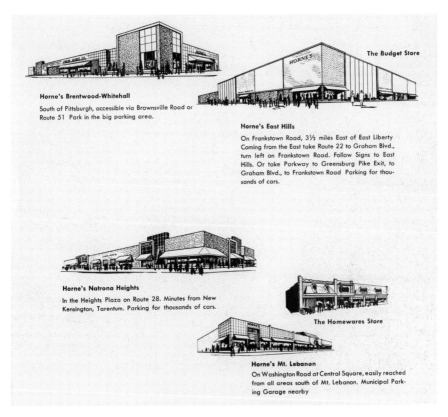

The Budget Store

Horne's Brentwood-Whitehall
South of Pittsburgh, accessible via Brownsville Road or Route 51 Park in the big parking area.

Horne's East Hills
On Frankstown Road, 3½ miles East of East Liberty Coming from the East take Route 22 to Graham Blvd., turn left on Frankstown Road. Follow Signs to East Hills. Or take Parkway to Greensburg Pike Exit, to Graham Blvd., to Frankstown Road Parking for thousands of cars.

Horne's Natrona Heights
In the Heights Plaza on Route 28. Minutes from New Kensington, Tarentum. Parking for thousands of cars.

The Homewares Store

Horne's Mt. Lebanon
On Washington Road at Central Square, easily reached from all areas south of Mt. Lebanon. Municipal Parking Garage nearby

This advertisement for Horne's suburban stores includes driving directions and parking information. Free parking was a perk of shopping in suburbia.

store of specialized shops covering two floors and a mezzanine and included a Budget Store and a Designer Salon. Like the other mall stores, Horne's Greengate was faced with white glazed brick and stone, and ceramic tile in "Horne's Blue" was used in the signage.

A highlight of the store's interior was a hanging sculpture by Pittsburgh artist Virgil Cantini. Called *Sky Scape*, the glass, steel and bronze sculpture measured twenty by twelve by sixteen feet and was suspended from the ceiling of the escalator well.

A mailer to local residents announcing the new store said that Horne's was delighted to be their new neighbor and invited them to open a Horne's charge account if they didn't already have one.

Horne's South Hills Village store, opened on July 28, 1965, was similar to the store at Greengate. It also covered two levels and was designed as a store of specialized shops, including a beauty shop, the specialty shop Fads n Frills and a Varsity Shop. At 190,000 square feet, Horne's South Hills village was the largest suburban store. It also included a Cantini sculpture over the escalator well. Called *The New Horizon*, the piece included fifty colored glass triangles and 1,000 feet of wrought-iron rods.

Children who were taken shopping at Horne's South Hills Village were likely to remember the shoe department. They could sit in a yellow scaled-down version of a pre-1935 trolley car to have their shoes fitted. Babies and toddlers had their shoes fitted in a nearby wooden "depot."

By the 1960s, the branch stores were holding special events just like the downtown Horne's, and newspaper advertising highlighted branch store sales. For many Horne's shoppers in the suburbs, the branch stores were almost as beloved as the downtown store. In 1960, Horne's managers were also champions of suburban stores; when reporting the store's highest sales in April 1960, they credited the performance of the suburban branch stores.

One of the biggest appeals of the suburban branch stores was the abundant free parking. Downtown Horne's, like other department stores, tried to provide parking for its suburban customers. In 1959, Horne's added a six-level downtown parking garage, and a 1961 advertisement claimed that "parking is no problem when you shop at Horne's." Shoppers were advised that they could park in one garage with an Arcade entrance into the store, have their car parked for them in another or conveniently park at a third option. The ad didn't mention how much parking would cost.

Parking rates were already an issue when the City of Pittsburgh passed a parking tax in December 1962. Bernard Horne, representing the chamber of commerce, was quoted in the press referencing a study of downtown department store shopping. The study had found that parking rates were already high enough to discourage downtown shopping. Retailers were resigned to the tax, which was passed. As much as shoppers liked the free parking in the suburbs, the branch stores didn't offer the breadth of merchandise or the services that were available downtown.

Horne's downtown bridal salon was popular across the region. "After he asks the question, you, the Bride-to-Be, will have many questions of your own. Let Horne's answer them all," a booklet for brides suggested. A store-wide bridal promotion in April 1950 was typical. Harkening back to the famous bridal windows of the 1920s, the bridal party and the trousseau were featured in Horne's windows. In the Bridal Studio, a bridal secretary would help the bride plan everything from bridal portraits, taken in the portrait studio, of course, to suggestions for the new house from the Home

Planning Center. There was a Bridal Fashion Show with clothing for the bride and groom, mother of the bride and the attendants. Wedding guests were encouraged to buy their finery at Horne's.

In 1952, Horne's published a small booklet for brides, "Your Guide to a Perfect Wedding." It listed all of the services the store had to offer brides. In addition to the bridal fashions, invitations and the predictable gifts in the bridal registry—china, silver, linens and glass—it directed the bride-to-be to other services. Horne's could provide a sewing consultant to the bride making her own gown, the Personal Service Bureau could help friends plan the bridal showers and the store bakery could make the wedding cake. If the bride had heirloom lace, Horne's could add it to the gown or use it as a cap or veil. The store also provided brides with information on how to plan a trousseau.

Horne's also distributed a baby care book for its customers in the early 1950s, as well as booklets with a list of layette requirements for babies. The book was actually a catalogue of baby supplies, including an early type of disposable diaper. And while the suburban stores all carried children's clothing, the finest clothing was only available downtown. The Cradle Corner sold handmade dresses from Marcella Julien, "The Paris House of Haute Couture for Children." Dresses in infant and toddler sizes ranged in price from $29.95 to $150.00; separate slips were $29.50. "For you who appreciate fine things, for you who feel that a tiny girl's first dress-up frock is as sentimentally important as her wedding gown." Horne's asked Marcella Julien for a list of current Pittsburgh customers, including those from the Mellon, Byers, Heinz, Robinson and Jones families, so that it could alert them that they no longer needed to travel to Paris for their daughters' dress-up frocks.

Those in search of adult fashion also needed to travel downtown. After the Depression and World War II, French fashion returned with a vengeance; the "New Look" celebrated prosperity, with its long hems and voluminous skirts that weren't possible with rationed cloth. Leading French designers began sending representatives to the United States, as they had done before 1930. Women's clothing had now segmented into departments by age group, starting with misses clothing and then juniors. Reliable sizing made shopping easier since it required fewer alterations.

Horne's continued to position itself as a fashion authority. Fashion Director Edith Shaw Stewart regularly attended fashion openings in Paris and London and provided commentary during fashion shows in the store. The local press included fashion information from Horne's in shopping columns like "Shopping with Polly," and the fashion editor at the *Pittsburgh Press*, Barbara Cloud, regularly reported Horne's fashion news.

Fashion shows were regular events in the downtown store. In May 1951, Esther Williams, representing Cole of California, was the guest commentator at the show Fashions for Outdoor Fun. Admission to the show was by ticket only, and tickets were only for women; a sign at the event proclaimed "For Women Only" as bathing suits were modeled. The same year, Horne's held a Millinery Fashion Show.

In the downstairs store, there were shows of spring fashion and back-to-school clothing. Upstairs, there were shows for businesswomen and for home sewers who used *Vogue* patterns.

Teen fashion had emerged in the late 1930s, and department stores began to court teens with fashion shows of their own. Horne's held a fashion show for teens in 1950 with its Soda Set Circus of Fashion. The store used the "Soda Set" designation for shows of retail fashion throughout the 1950s. In April 1956, it also held a High School Fashion Show where girls modeled the outfits they had made themselves.

Horne's emphasis on fashion extended to home sewers. The store teamed with *Vogue* for decades, selling patterns and displaying fashion in its fabric department.

By the 1960s, Horne's was collaborating with *Seventeen* magazine to produce its annual fall fashion show for teens. In 1963, the store ran a sixteen-page fashion spread in the August issue of *Seventeen*, and an advertisement for the show included a line drawing of a girl in plaid culottes and knee socks wearing a vest, a long-sleeved shirt, a scarf and a small cap. That year, Horne's college shop was called Saville Row Joe's College Haberdashery.

In addition to its fashion shows in the store, Horne's took its shows on the road, providing entertainment for women's clubs and for charity events. There were fashion shows at the PAA and for the Junior League at the University Club. A May 1965 swimsuit fashion show in Mount Lebanon was open to the public, unlike its 1951 counterpart.

In 1965, Horne's began what would become its signature fashion event, the Symphony Fashion Gala. The event was announced in July 1965 as the latest benefit planned by the Women's Association of the Pittsburgh Symphony Society. Held on September 15 at Carnegie Music Hall, the event was "an introduction into the fall fashion scene as seen by the Joseph Horne Co., which will coordinate the show." Jane Vandermade, Horne's fashion director, produced the annual event during the 1960s.

The Symphony Gala included appearances by leading international fashion designers, beginning in 1965 with Adele Simpson, who also visited Horne's. In 1966, Jean Patou was the guest, and 1,100 women watched as he launched a new perfume, "Caline," at the gala. Bill Blass was the celebrity guest in 1967 when 1,300 people watched the show on September 27, which was followed by a champagne reception. Valentino appeared in 1968, when the gala show was followed by high tea. And on September 26, 1969, Donald Brooks, Geoffrey Beene and Oscar de la Renta headlined the annual Symphony Fashion Gala.

While Horne's scheduled events in its suburban stores, larger events were limited to the flagship downtown store. An events calendar during the 1950s lists a home sewing promotion with *Seventeen*, a tree-planting event, celebration of UN Day, sewing clinics for home economics teachers and display of a miniature amusement park in the toy department. The miniature park, made by Glenshaw resident Frank Salisbury, was twenty-eight feet long and four feet wide and needed four motors to run the tiny rides.

In 1950, Horne's started its annual Tulip Show, with thousands of blooming tulips flown in from Holland; visitors could order bulbs of the forty-one varieties, which would be shipped in time for fall planting. A silhouette cutter also came every spring to do children's portraits. In June 1952, Horne's hosted the Industrial Progress exhibit, presented by the

Horne's was famous across the region for its annual Symphony Fashion Gala, which brought leading designers to Pittsburgh.

Henry Ford Museum and Greenfield Village and supported by a group of national industries. Among the twenty exhibits displayed in the Assembly Hall, visitors could see the chair in which Lincoln was assassinated.

In May 1953, Horne's also began its Annual Youth Day, where local high school students shadowed store executives for a day. Students interested

Horne's often hosted the Pittsburgh Pirates for events in the store. Pirates signing autographs in this undated photograph appear to be Dick Stuart on the left, Roberto Clemente in the left center and Bill Mazeroski on the far right.

in retail careers were recruited at the event. In April, Mickey Mantle and Johnny Mize had taken time off from the exhibition game they were playing at Forbes Field to autograph books in Horne's book department.

In 1958, Horne's set up an indoor roller skating rink in the store for kids to use during the summer. The first day, so many people came to the event that the police had to be called to control the crowds, but the crowds tapered off with the opening of the Allegheny County Fair. The following year, Horne's decided to repeat the event, providing free skating for children sixteen and under from June 20 until August 8. For children who didn't have their own rink skates, Horne's provided clamp skates. In addition to the free skating, there were regular shows by the Lou Tesla Follies.

The children weren't the only ones who appreciated the free summer entertainment. A customer, wife of a steelworker, sent the store a note: "One of the nicest things I've heard in years is Horne's having the summer roller skating for children. We have curtailed all unnecessary spending pending the

During the summer of 1958, Horne's set up an indoor roller skating rink where teenagers like these could skate in air-conditioned comfort.

outcome of the steel strike, but believe me, when I'm busy again, I'll shop Horne's as much as possible."

The range of store events in 1959 included Ernie's Miniature Circus in the toy department, where Aunt Jemima also visited to show shoppers how to make pancakes on miniature baking sets. During Fun Week, also in the toy department, Josie Carey and Fred Rogers visited with the *Children's Corner* people from WQED. There was a fishing clinic in Sporting Goods with films about sport in Canada and Alaska.

In 1959, Alaska became a state, and Horne's had a native totem pole carver in the store, where he carved miniature totem poles. He also visited local schools, where children thought that he lived in an igloo and ate walrus meat. Pittsburgh also celebrated its bicentennial in 1959, and Horne's used a bicentennial theme "Pittsburgh's Contributions to the World" across the store. There were bicentennial windows, bicentennial lunches in the tearoom and eighteenth-century military uniforms displayed as part of a British Heritage exhibit. In November, Horne's presented the "biggest birthday cake" to the city.

In 1959, when racial stereotypes were more accepted, a model portraying "Aunt Jemima" made pancakes in Horne's toy department to demonstrate kids' cooking sets.

The events required full-time staff to plan and implement them. Horne's, like most department stores, was still generating profits in the 1960s, so it didn't curtail events in the downtown store. A month-long calendar of events for January 1963 lists Bishop Method Sewing Classes, a Bridal Fashion Show, a charity fashion show and a Public Safety Show, along with Warehouse

Clearance and January White Sales. Eva Gabor appeared at Horne's during the premier of U.S. Steel's film *Rhapsody in Steel* at the Hilton. Horne's hung a banner outside the store to mark the event, and inside shoppers could visit steel exhibits, including the preview of a 1963 Buick Riviera.

Two ponies from Schenley Park also visited Horne's in 1963, providing almost two thousand free pony rides in the Assembly Hall on the seventh floor. They were part of an Animal Land event that also included birds and rabbits.

In addition to the annual Tulip Show, Horne's sponsored a Bonsai Show and a Flower Fragrance Fair, where flower arrangements, using 125,000 blossoms, interpreted different perfumes in the store windows and the cosmetics department. For several years, Horne's also hosted Japanese flower arrangers during its annual Ikebana Flower Arranging event. Garden clubs were invited to attend; following the event, they could buy containers designed for Ikebana in the store.

There was a two-week-long Pennsylvania Dutch Folk Festival, a "Miss Smile" competition sponsored by Janzen and visits by "Miss Wool," who arrived with twenty-seven suitcases of clothing to model. Williamsburg craftspeople came to demonstrate their skills in making wigs, candles and paper. A space exhibit in the Men's Store used models from NASA to show how man would land on the moon.

World's Fairs were popular department store events; Horne's apparently held its first in 1961 with demonstrations of European crafts. The next year, Horne's was serving "Foreign Foods" in the tearoom and advertising foreign fashion and housewares. Foreign issues of *Vogue* were on display, with a preview of new 1963 fashions. Visitors could see a scale model of La Scala and watch European craftspeople carve wooden shoes, make ships in bottles, pour candles and tool leather.

For the World's Fair in October 1963, Horne's displayed English tavern signs, a collection of antique miniature chests, a replica of Milan Cathedral and Italian fashion in the windows. One window showcased a collection of brass horns: "We view them as a symbol of Horne's voice in seeking out the best the world has to offer for its customers." Inside there was a pavilion of world interiors and imported goods on sale throughout the store.

Classes and workshops were always popular events. They were held in the suburban stores—both Northway and South Hills Horne's hosted "Debbie Drake" fitness classes in 1965. There was a charge for the fitness course, but Horne's provided the equipment, which it offered for sale.

Authors often visited Horne's book department during the 1950s. Here the Kovels sign one of their popular books on antiques.

Downtown, shoppers could attend Charles H. Goren lectures on bridge; gourmet cooking classes with Mme. Dione Lucas, who provided recipes with her instruction; and a school for turkey callers and hunter safety courses during the four-day Sportsmen's Show. For sewers, there were Bishop Method classes, as well as courses in Advanced Dressmaking, Costume Design and Patternmaking and Custom Made Millinery. For those who weren't as accomplished, there was a Saturday morning class, Dressmaking for Beginners.

Teenagers were welcomed at regular Seventeen Beauty Workshops, a series of seven two-hour sessions on Saturdays that focused on good grooming, make-up and posture. There was a three-dollar charge for the class, and they apparently filled quickly.

For younger children, four to six, the store held "Horne's Music Kindergarten" in its Keyboard Center at Gateway 2. Again, there was a charge, but the store provided the pianos. Children without a piano at home could take lessons, and if they were interested in continuing, Horne's would

Horne's Music Kindergarten introduced children to the piano in its keyboard department in Gateway 2. For children who wanted to continue instruction, the store was happy to sell instruments to parents.

advise parents on choosing an instrument. Horne's Music Center used a similar approach by offering guitar classes in August 1966. The classes were called "Horne's-a-balloo," a rift on the popular TV show *Hullaballoo*.

It wasn't the only case where TV influenced merchandising. Television now replaced movies in popular culture as more and more families had sets at home. In July 1950, Horne's had invited customers to watch the All-Star baseball game in "Cool Comfort" in its seventh-floor Assembly Hall, where a battery of television sets made every seat a box seat. The store was also supplementing its radio advertising with television, sponsoring *Uncle Miltie's TV Christmas Party* on Christmas afternoon, televised on WDTV. On November 1, 1952, it sponsored local election returns on WDTV; later in November, Horne's advertised Westinghouse TVs for sale and provided approved service agencies for installing televisions in "outlying areas."

Television also inspired children's toys. By May 1955, Horne's had a Davy Crockett Trading Post in the store. For the opening of the new Youth

Floor, author Enid LaMonte Meadowcroft was autographing her children's book *The Story of Davy Crockett*, assisted by Davy in costume, who handed out balloons. Parents shopping for children could buy "Howdy Doody Jiffyalls," overalls with convenient zippers down the front.

Television celebrities also visited the toy department. In the early 1950s, Zippy the Chimp from *The Howdy Doody Show* performed at Horne's. Huckleberry Hound, Yogi Bear and Quick Draw McGraw visited shortly before the 1960 presidential election. Customers were invited to come, shake the candidates' hands, listen to campaign speeches and vote "Huckleberry Hound for President." Four years later, Shari Lewis and her puppets presented a show in the toy department.

Local television celebrities also visited Horne's. Josie Carey and Fred Rogers attended the 1955 Toy Fair, where Robert the Robot was the master of ceremonies. Carey and Rogers returned in December 1959 to autograph their latest phonograph album, *Tomorrow on the Children's Corner*. Ten songs on each side of the record told a story about King Friday the Thirteenth. In the spring of 1968, Marie Torre broadcast her morning interview show from the Horne's tearoom, and customers were invited to come and watch.

Zippy the Chimp from the hugely popular *Howdy Doody Show* performed at Horne's in the 1950s.

Robert the Robot was the master of ceremonies at the 1955 Toy Fair in the Horne's toy department.

Fred Rogers also hosted a short-lived children's program on WTAE in 1965. The fifteen-minute show, sponsored by Horne's, was canceled after six months because Mr. Rogers was uncomfortable doing advertising segments for toys.

By September 1962, Horne's was offering color TVs on sale; at $500 to $700 each, they were still expensive for many families. The small, portable TVs on sale in October 1965 were more affordable.

The store was also offering new services. A downtown mending shop would re-weave damaged fabric, repair zippers and handbags and clean suede and leather. Suburban shoppers could drop off and pick up items for repair at their local Horne's branch. The store would remove, clean and service air conditioners in the fall, store them over the winter and re-install them in the spring. Customers could contact Horne's Servicemaster for cleaning furniture, carpets or a whole house.

By the 1960s, many things at Horne's had stayed the same. The store was still selling silver, fine linens, china and crystal. It was still offering fur storage and advertising spring hats. It was still advertising girdles for bowling, golf, tennis and swimming.

But some things were changing. Hems were rising on the women in the store advertisements. The graphics in those ads were becoming more modish. In one advertisement from March 1968, Horne's even alluded to the social unrest across the country. "Horne's demonstrates against work," the advertisement for time-saving kitchen electronics read. "Joseph Horne Co is now sponsoring demonstrations with a difference...they are the helpful, constructive kind."

The venerable metal Charga-Plates were now being made of plastic, and customers were given extra months to make each payment, recognition perhaps that charge customers were vital, comprising 74 percent of the store's customers.

In 1957, Horne's began using UPS to provide delivery services; a city-wide strike of delivery drivers in 1950 that challenged department stores may have affected the decision.

In 1965, the store's North Side warehouse was sold for development of a new stadium. A new warehouse covering ten acres was built in the Chartiers Valley Industrial Park to serve all eight Horne's stores; shoppers would no longer be able to board a store bus downtown and ride to the annual Warehouse Sale.

Because employees were using it less and less and it was expensive to maintain, Horne's leased Camp Horne to Ohio Township for use as a public park. In 1966, the store was considering an offer from the Avonworth Municipal Authority to buy Camp Horne, an offer it would ultimately accept.

But perhaps the biggest change didn't appear that significant at the time. After months of rumors that Horne's was going to be sold, the president announced that the store was joining the Associated Dry Goods Corporation. Based in New York, the corporation was a consortium of fifty-seven national department stores; the largest was Lord & Taylor. At the end of the announcement, made at a special employee meeting, the audience applauded, and veteran employees quoted in the press called the move "wonderful." While Horne's and Associated Dry Goods would exchange stock, store management would remain in charge and store policies would not change. Employees were relieved to know that their benefits weren't changing.

Their relief was to be short-lived. The next three decades would prove challenging for the department store industry in general as well as for the department stores in Pittsburgh.

From Horne's to Lazarus

D uring its first century, Horne's had faced many challenges—fire, flood, four wars and at least three financial depressions. But the challenges of the 1970s would affect the department store industry in general. Severe inflation early in the decade drove shoppers to buy on price, not necessarily by choice. Food prices had risen dramatically, but food was a necessity—department store merchandise was not.

Cash-strapped consumers now had a new retail choice: the discount store. Discounters would morph into the ubiquitous big-box stores of the 2000s, but in the 1970s they were relatively new. Unlike traditional department stores, they weren't located in urban downtowns, but in the suburbs. There were no clerks to wait on customers; customers were expected to wait on themselves. All of the registers were located in the front of the store, and the employees at those registers were likely to be part-timers. Since the discount industry was male-dominated, there weren't as many career opportunities for women.

With the passage of the Consumer Goods Pricing Act in 1975, all restraint was removed from pricing, an advantage to the discounters. Department stores that offered higher-quality merchandise weren't as affected as much as stores with lower-quality merchandise because higher-priced items weren't offered at the discounters. In response to the discounters, department stores merged to become part of larger chains. But such a merger in the 1970s didn't result in loss of local identity. When Associated Dry Goods acquired Horne's in 1972, most local shoppers were unaware of the change in ownership. The new owner expanded throughout the region, adding Horne's stores in Erie, Pennsylvania, and northeast Ohio.

To shoppers, Horne's looked much like it had during the previous decades. The store was still selling sterling silver and Oriental rugs, although by 1977, it was offering a twenty-month payment plan with no interest to those buying at least $100 worth of silver, crystal or china. There was a Williamsburg Shop on the fifth floor with other gift shops. While the furniture galleries were re-designed in 1977, they were still selling traditional solid-wood furniture. And television was still influencing the toy department. For Christmas 1977, shoppers there could find a Big Red Trolley toy from *Mr. Roger's Neighborhood* with Daniel Striped Tiger and Lady Elaine Fairchilde aboard. The trolley played "It's a Beautiful Day in the Neighborhood."

There were new items for sale as well. By 1976, Horne's was selling digital watches and pocket calculators from Texas Instruments. It was demonstrating and selling microwave ovens. In March 1976, the store advertised that it was the first in Pittsburgh to carry the Betamax system, "New from Sony." By the end of 1979, in "Horne's Bright New World of Home Video," shoppers could receive a $100 "Don't Wait Rebate" on an RCA SelectaVision® VCR, regularly priced at $1,099. "Record any program while you're asleep or away, record one program while you watch another, or record the program you're watching, and be able to see it again and again."

For those interested in the recent revival of pierced earrings, Horne's had a registered nurse visit the store to safely pierce customers' ears. The $7.50 fee included a first pair of pierced earrings.

Activities continued in the store as well. By 1970, Horne's had renamed its Assembly Hall the Special Events Center, and special events scheduled in the downtown store were often repeated at select branches in the suburbs, often those located in shopping malls. The *Seventeen* beauty classes were rebranded as *Seventeen* Beautyworks for girls in the ninth to twelfth grades and a sub-teen course on good grooming added for girls in the seventh and eighth grades. In addition to the classes that were traditionally held downtown, the courses were offered at Beaver Valley, Greengate and Monroeville Malls.

The March 1971 *Seventeen* Fashion Show, where "The Pinto Beans will set the beat," was still held only downtown on a Saturday afternoon. But five years later, the show was held not just downtown but also in five suburban branches, all located in malls. A "Wolfman Jack at Horne's" event played five suburban malls during the evening before coming downtown on a Saturday. The event included a fashion show, music and prizes, including T-shirt

Horne's teamed with *Seventeen* magazine on fashion events downtown and at its suburban locations. In the 1970s, the "peasant look" was the rage.

giveaways, and attracted crowds at Monroeville, Greengate, Northway, Beaver Valley and Southern Park malls.

In addition to larger events, Horne's hosted events tied to merchandising in individual departments. In February 1970, the fashion fabric department hosted representatives from different manufacturers for a daylong "Make It" event for teens. They could learn how to sew, how to work with knit fabrics, how to make simple clothing and accessories from scarves and how to make things using buttons and trims. In May, Johnny Whitaker, "Jody" from the TV show *Family Affair*, was visiting South Hills Village and Monroeville Mall to promote a line of boys' clothing. In 1979, the Pittsburgh Doll Club exhibited some of its collection and sponsored a talk on collecting dolls by local author John Axe, who would autograph his books in the doll department. The department not only included dolls for children but also collectible porcelain and Madame Alexander dolls for adults.

Throughout the 1970s, the Horne's book department was also hosting authors for autographing events: Bennett Cerf, Hugh Downs, Erma Bombeck and Stefan Lorant. In February 1975, Roy Blunt was in the store to autograph his book *About Three Bricks Shy of a Load* along with Andy Russell and Ray Mansfield, who were also signing autographs. In 1976, Horne's was still organizing Book and Author Dinners.

Events also reflected national issues. In May 1970, those who missed the first Earth Day display in Horne's windows downtown could still visit it. The corner window had been turned into a "walk-through," starting in the cosmetics department. Visitors could see a crushed car—apparently a new way of handling junk cars instead of just dumping them in a lake or river. The display, developed by students in the Carnegie Mellon design department, also included an incinerating toilet to reduce water use. It encouraged people to avoid leaded gasoline, carpool to reduce pollution from exhaust and avoid colored paper napkins because the dyes harmed the environment.

President Nixon's historic trip to China was also reflected in an October 1970 sale of Chinese antiques called the "Friendship Collection." It included jade, porcelain and antique jewelry at prices ranging from $15 to $25,000; select items were also on sale at Monroeville Mall and South Hills Village.

But shoppers who were paying attention would also notice changes at the store. By 1971, almost all of the fabric sold in the store was synthetic. The new Miss Horne Shop, opened in August 1970, was for "Miss Horne, our independent, non-wealthy young friend....The one who holds down a good job or does a lot to help her husband hold down his. Or both." Shops were located downtown and in branch stores and seemed to reflect a new reality driven by the economy of the 1970s: more and more women were working, not just before marrying and settling down, but out of necessity to support themselves or their families.

Horne's now held more and more sales, some of them just at individual suburban stores, where there were "acres of free parking...at your favorite suburban Horne's." For many suburban shoppers, the local branch

In May 1970, CMU students turned Horne's windows into an environmental exhibit that included this crushed car.

Horne's saluted the presidential race in 1972 by featuring candidate Archie Bunker in one of its windows.

was their favorite Horne's, as fewer and fewer of them had the time or inclination to travel downtown to shop. To lure shoppers to the main store in November 1978, Horne's offered them three hours of free parking at any Pittsburgh Parking Authority garage if they spent five dollars or more. A January 1971 advertisement for Horne's annual warehouse sale, now held at its new warehouse, included a map so that shoppers could find the new site and advertised thirteen and a half acres of free parking. Buses ran from the downtown store at thirty-minute intervals for those who didn't want to drive.

Horne's was now regularly open in the evenings and on Sundays. An advertisement in 1978 notified shoppers of the Sunday hours, and in 1979, the store was open for holiday shopping from 11:00 a.m. to 6:00 p.m. downtown and at five suburban malls on Sundays. Not only was there less commitment to the Sabbath on the part of the public, but people who worked all week, including more and more women, were also only able to shop on the weekends. Still, the Sunday hours were a temporary holiday measure.

In 1978, the Horne's tearoom shut its doors, and in November, all of the equipment and fixtures from the store's central bakery were offered at public auction.

If the 1970s were a challenge, the 1980s were worse. The stagnant economy continued and, combined with other factors, devastated the steel industry. The steel industry had supported the middle-class way of life in the region, allowing not only those who worked in the mills to prosper but also industries and services that supported those workers. By January 1983, unemployment in Pittsburgh had reached 17.1 percent, and 212,000 people were out of work. The numbers were even higher in the surrounding counties: 19.5 percent in Armstrong County, served by Horne's Natrona Heights branch, and 27.1 percent in Beaver County, where the store's Beaver Valley Mall branch was located. The numbers for Beaver County were actually higher than peak U.S. unemployment in the Great Depression.

Mills closed across the region. U.S. Steel closed the Duquesne and Clairton Works in 1984, followed by the Homestead Works in 1986 and National Tube and American Bridge in 1987. By 1985, LTV's Aliquippa Works and South Side Works were almost idle; the company had laid off 8,000 workers at Aliquippa in 1984. Between 1979 and 1987, the region lost 133,000 manufacturing jobs, and the population in the city of Pittsburgh dropped by 30 percent While average millworkers may not have been regular Horne's shoppers, the collapse of the industry also affected the managers within the steel companies and the professional and service class that supported steel.

In the retail industry, department stores felt increased pressure from chain stores that expanded across the country, and more and more of them merged to fight the chains. Now the mergers were starting to result in the loss of distinctive store brands, fewer shopping choices and less local flavor. National brands dominated the merchandise available to shoppers.

For Horne's, the turmoil caused by mergers added to the challenge of a distressed local economy. In 1986, May Company acquired Associated Dry Goods. May already owned cross-town department store rival Kaufmann's, and local business leaders doubted that May would operate both stores in downtown Pittsburgh and in regional malls. The City of Pittsburgh and Allegheny County both protested the merger to the Federal Trade Commission, and editorials in the local press supported the protest. The sale went through anyway, and a group of local investors, Maverick Management Company (MMC), bought Horne's from the May Company, which continued to own and operate Kaufmann's.

MMC was an investment company. Since Horne's was profitable, the investment company entertained several offers from entities that were interested in buying the store. Most of the deals fell through quickly, but one in 1988 seemed destined to happen. Mall developer Edward DeBartolo from Youngstown, Ohio, and department store chain Dillard's created a partnership to buy Horne's. Again, the sale had to be approved by the Federal Trade Commission since both Horne's and Dillard's, now owner of Higbee's, had stores in northeastern Ohio. The FTC granted approval to the sale, and a date was set for the formal purchase.

On July 30, 1988, Horne's president, Robert O'Connell, announced that the store was not going through with the sale. Employees were told that the purchase, scheduled to occur by July 31, had been delayed. For many of them, it was a reprieve. Hundreds had received layoff notices, and one sales clerk commented, "There's just been so many rumors, you don't know."

The Horne's store president acknowledged that the biggest impact to the store had been uncertainty for the store's employees. Between 480 and 550 people had been told that their jobs would be eliminated and that they would be laid off. Many of them were buyers; Dillard's already had buyers in place, and they would be doing the buying for both stores. While no one was actually laid off, between 75 and 100 employees had voluntarily left for new jobs. Dillard's had installed its own accounting and sales systems and had trained employees on them. They had developed and scheduled new advertisements. They had also intended to take over inventory purchasing, so fourth-quarter purchasing was behind schedule.

But the Horne's president assured the press that the store would make up for lost time.

On August 2, 1988, just days after the aborted sale, the store president announced that its top priority was a return to normal.

In many ways, Horne's had continued to operate as normal in spite of the uncertainty. "Mean Joe Greene" was at the downtown store on October 11, 1980, where shoppers could "have a smile and a Coke with the man who's won everyone's heart in his award-winning commercial." Mean Joe would sign autographed photos from the Coke commercials and answer questions. He also donated five of his own jerseys for a prize drawing.

In March 1984, the store held a *Seventeen* Fashion Show, was taking applications for its Teen Fashion Board and was offering breakfast with the Easter Bunny, presumably at Josephine's since it had replaced the Horne's tearoom. In July 1985, tennis player John McEnroe was in the store autographing photographs for Haggar. The next year, there was a Kid's Day at the downtown store and five malls on a fall Saturday. There were Halloween masks to color and Halloween lollipops. Children could participate in a Hug-a-Bear contest where the winner would be the child who could hold the most bears. Pittsburgh Steeler Mike Merriweather was on hand to sign autographs in Monroeville. Children enrolled in Horne's Kid's Club would receive 10 percent off the merchandise their parents bought.

By the late 1980s, Horne's was still offering the *Seventeen* Beautyworks classes and holding a warehouse sale. There was a spring fashion show at the Monroeville branch and a fashion show of cocktail, dinner and evening clothes downtown. A Royal Doulton shop opened in Horne's downtown in time for Christmas in 1987 with a ribbon-cutting ceremony and a tea to follow.

Horne's continued to store, repair and re-fashion furs and would take old furs as trade-ins for new ones. In October 1980, Christmas purchases made on the store's credit card could be deferred for payment the next March.

In 1982, anyone purchasing an Atari® gaming system would receive an Atari® jacket. The system was on sale for $159; it included a TV switch, AC adapter, two sets of controllers to work from a chair and the Combat Game Program, with twenty-seven games on one cartridge. Additional games were also for sale: video pinball, Circus Atari® or PacMan from $26.95 to $37.95. Rory the Atari Robot would be visiting the Horne's stores at South Hills Village and Monroeville Thursday and Friday evenings.

And for those interested in the latest telephone technology, there were TouchTone® phones and a cordless phone that could be used outside. Both phones were available with a redial feature.

In 1980, Horne's even tried to get the state's Liquor Control Board to lease space in its store to sell wine and liquor that was only available by special order in the state stores. The deal didn't go through. Horne's president, Joseph Vales, was quoted in the local press as noting, "We thought we were providing a public service. The idea was to give people the opportunity to buy a decent bottle of wine."

Horne's also continued to expand and upgrade its stores in spite of threats of an Associated Dry Goods/May merger. In 1986, when the merger was announced, Horne's was planning new stores in Ross Park Mall and Century III Mall as well as in Cleveland. The company president publically announced that the plans would be moving forward.

The new stores were part of an ongoing program of store improvement, particularly in the suburbs. In September 1981, the store at Northway was refurbished and debuted to the public with a three-day sale. There were demonstrations throughout the store, and Steeler L.C. Greenway was on hand to sign autographs on Friday evening.

In September 1985, the "Newly Glamorized" store at South Hills Village had its début with three days of special events. There was a chocolate festival where shoppers could learn how to make truffles and how to make chocolates with a microwave. Horne's had a Talking Scale in the store, and shoppers were invited to guess their own weight. The person who guessed closest to his or her own weight on the Talking Scale would win that weight in chocolate. Steeler Louis Lipps was on hand to autograph cards for Nike.

Adding to the glamour, a new Ralph Lauren Home Furnishing Shop opened at Horne's South Hills Village. For the event, the store was selling one-of-a-kind Waterford crystal lamps that ranged in price from $1,300 to $2,650.

In October 1986, the new stores at Ross Park Mall and Century III Mall were opened to the public with formal ribbon-cutting ceremonies. Local high school bands and radio personalities provided the entertainment. The store at Ross Park sold only clothing and accessories, and Horne's retained its store in Northway Mall for home furnishings and housewares. In 1987, the store at the Monroeville Mall was renovated and dubbed the "New Horne's Monroeville."

In keeping with the upgrades, the department store changed its name in its advertising from the Joseph Horne Company to the simpler Horne's. It also developed a new logo, a pair of stylized intertwined horns.

Horne's got a publicity boost from its appearance on film. The branch store in the Monroeville Mall was featured in the 1978 George Romero horror film *Dawn of the Dead*, sequel to the classic *Night of the Living Dead*. In the sequel, the zombies invade a shopping mall.

The downtown store was used as the location for a 1987 thriller *Lady Beware*. In the film, the main character, a beautiful young woman, works as a window dresser for the store. Unlike those in the staid, conservative real-life store, her windows featured sexy, slightly kinky themes. While she is working in the windows, she attracts the attention of a handsome and very married psychopathic stalker. He follows her home to her loft apartment decorated with store mannequins and lingerie. He watches her as she bathes by candlelight, thinking of new and more provocative themes for her windows. Finally, the stalker begins calling her on the phone and intercepting her mail. When she reports him to his wife, he comes to the store in a rage, intent on killing her. The film culminates with a scene on the store roof underneath the illuminated Horne's logo and sign.

By the mid-1980s, Horne's was financially sound; 1985 sales were $209 million, with earnings before taxes of $12 million. There were ten stores in the Pittsburgh area: downtown, Beaver Valley Mall, Natrona Heights, Ross Park, Northway Mall, Monroeville Mall, Greengate Mall, Century III Mall, South Hills Village and Brentwood/Whitehall. Regional stores included two

In the mid-1980s, Horne's formally changed its name and developed a new logo, the two entwined horns seen on this delivery truck.

in Erie, Pennsylvania, West Erie and Millcreek Mall; a store in Youngstown, Ohio; and two in Cleveland, Randall Park and Mentor. A third store was planned for Westgate, Ohio, in 1987.

But there were also casualties. The Whitehall store was converted to a clearance center, and the East Hills store was closed. After it had sat vacant for several years, it became a warehouse for a vinyl window manufacturer. At some point, Horne's also closed the Fads and Frills Shop in the Pittsburgh Airport. When the new airport opened with its nationally recognized Airmall, Horne's was not among the shops.

Horne's also reduced the operating hours for its downtown store in January 1988. As part of a community-wide effort to get suburbanites to stay in town after work and shop, Horne's had extended its hours to 7:00 p.m. three days a week two years earlier. There was so little business that the later hours weren't justified. Other stores were also reducing their evening hours, and the press noted that downtown retail had been hard hit by the shutdown of Gulf Oil, layoffs at major corporations, the closing of Gimbels and construction projects that made it harder for people to come into the city from the suburbs. Horne's was still open until 9:00 p.m. on Monday and Thursday nights.

The same year, Horne's announced that it was canceling plans to open a new store at Severance Center in Cleveland Heights. That store had been scheduled to open in November 1988.

By the end of the decade, Horne's was pulling out all of the stops to get shoppers into the downtown store for Christmas shopping. It was open from 10:00 a.m. until 11:00 p.m. on Sundays. There were free gift wrapping and free shopping bags. Shoppers could leave their purchases while they continued to shop and then pick everything up before leaving the store.

As Horne's entered the last decade of the twentieth century, the tumult of the 1980s wasn't readily apparent. In a March 1990 article in the local press, Jane Vandermade highlighted upcoming fashion shows, including a bridal show. Horne's would be celebrating an annual Daffodil Day to benefit the American Cancer Society. In Monroeville, Eileen Ford would be on hand as part of her 1990 Supermodel of the World Search. Local search finalists would be modeling. There was a scarf-tying demonstration, and shoppers who bought fashion jewelry from Monet, Trifari or Napier would get a free gift.

Horne's held bridal fairs in Monroeville, South Hills and downtown in conjunction with *Modern Bride* magazine. Representatives from Lenox and makers of crystal, silver and kitchen appliances were at the fair to demonstrate their products, and representatives from Horne's bridal registry helped brides chose items for their wish lists.

At Kid's Day in April, again in Monroeville, Hello Kitty showed parents how to fill an Easter basket without using eggs or candy. In November, the downtown store celebrated the third anniversary of the Royal Doulton Shop with figurines, character jugs and tableware on sale. In the Fashion Galleries, shoppers could find Anne Klein, Chanel and Jagger. In August 1993, the furniture department in Horne's South Hills Village moved out of the store and into its own standalone, twenty-thousand-square-foot building.

But there were hints of trouble. In January 1990, Horne's announced that it would no longer be staging the annual Symphony Gala fashion show. The event had been a fixture of the fall social season for twenty-five years and brought some of the world's most prestigious designers to Pittsburgh. After starting in 1965 at the Carnegie Music Hall, the show moved to Heinz Hall in 1971. In 1989, the gala raised $100,000 for the symphony; in twenty-five years, its total donation was more than $1 million.

Horne's said that its decision had nothing to do with money. "It was not a cost-cutting move," Jane Vandermade told the local press. As vice-president and fashion director for Horne's, she had been responsible for organizing and running the gala since its inception. The event took the store's fashion staff two months to produce, although the featured designer was often secured a year before the event.

To some, the end of the gala was not a complete surprise. During the DeBartolo/Dillard's acquisition discussions, many people wondered if the gala would end after 1988. Horne's fashion staff had been notified that they would be out of work if the acquisition went ahead since Dillard's did not have a fashion department. When the deal fell through, the twenty-fifth show in 1989 went ahead as originally planned. Designer Bill Blass came to Pittsburgh for his fifth appearance as featured designer.

In February 1992, Horne's announced a "huge loss" for the fiscal year, and the local press provided details. Apparently, the loss for the past fiscal year was almost as much as the combined losses during the previous two years. The losses were attributed to a tough retail climate, but there were other issues. The store had been hampered with debt following the aborted Debartolo/Dillard's acquisition. Horne's had tried to sell off most of its store and warehouse property in July 1991 to pay off the debt, but that deal also failed. The analysis also revealed that the store had not made a profit since 1986 and likely wouldn't make a profit until 1995. It was not good news.

Bill Blass was featured at multiple Symphony Fashion Galas.

Horne's was suing the two partners over the termination of the tentative 1986 agreement they had reached, and the analysis was prepared for the lawsuit. While Horne's was able to restructure its debt, it still felt that it had been damaged and that the failed agreement had affected its profitability.

In March 1992, Horne's announced that it was closing its bargain basement store downtown. The reason: it didn't have enough merchandise to sell at clearance since it had fewer stores. Horne's had sold its five Ohio stores to Dillard's as part of the ongoing legal battle. There were no immediate plans to reuse the basement space, but employees were offered other positions at the store.

During the summer of 1993, Federated Department Stores, a national chain, quietly approached Horne's about buying the store. There were no public announcements, but the rumor mill spread the story. On April 30, 1994, it was official: Federated would purchase Horne's, and the official closing of the deal would take place in May. The store would be part of Federated's Lazarus Division. An article noted that Horne's finances had improved but were still so bad than some manufacturers required payment before they would ship merchandise to the store.

Federated said that it was prepared to invest $66 million to refurbish the store and that 90 percent of the employees would retain their jobs. Nearly two hundred buyers and administrative staff would be laid off. One employee told the press, "There's a feeling of relief now. They now know what is going on. They [Federated] are going to pump money into the organization and make it stronger." The press noted optimistically that Federated would continue to carry many of the same national brands as Horne's and that the larger chain would be better able to compete with Kaufmann's.

In May 1994, Lazarus announced the upcoming layoffs: a total of 326 employees, not the 200 originally anticipated. They would include middle- and upper-level managers at the downtown store, buyers and assistant buyers, window designers and display staff, operations people, the accounts receivable department and, lastly, the finance and human resources departments. The layoffs would be phased over seven months. Some employees were offered the option to stay during the transition; they would be given a "retention bonus" in addition to their salaries. Michael Pulte, the last Horne's president, would be retiring in June.

Lazarus planned to have the new store signage in place by October. By Christmas 1994, Horne's would be identified as Lazarus. The new owners did say that they weren't sure if they would keep the downtown store open in its current location since they felt that most of the downtown activity was centered on Grant Street. The City of Pittsburgh said that it was prepared to offer financial incentives to keep the former Horne's flagship store open downtown.

Horne's downtown flagship store lasted a year under the Lazarus banner. It was closed on Christmas Eve 1995. On the last morning, there was no closeout sale, no rush of customers through the doors. Just a few customers came to say goodbye to the building or to their favorite salespeople; two hundred of them were to be laid off. Some customers took photographs. A salesman wore his old, blue Horne's name tag and a trumpet-patterned tie. At 5:40 p.m., a security guard put up a shield on the revolving door and the store was closed.

In January 1996, its fixtures were liquidated at auction. The building had been purchased by Blue Cross of Western Pennsylvania (now Highmark) for use as an office building. It planned to renovate the exterior and keep as much of the original interior as possible, while converting the first floor for modern retail. As the press noted at the time, the Horne's interior was the last classic-period department store interior remaining in the city, with its twenty-three-foot-high ceiling with gilded decorative plaster and its marble columns. Federated donated the store's records and photograph collection to the Historical Society of Western Pennsylvania. One of the iconic bronze plaques outside the store ended up at the John Heinz History Center's museum, and Blue Cross retained others outside the building. The Horne's logo of two entwined horns also remained in the pavement outside a store entrance.

Ironically, the new Lazarus store at Fifth Avenue and Wood Street closed after a few years in business. In 2005, Federated and Macy's merged, and Kaufmann's, Horne's cross-town rival, was converted to a Macy's. It was just like every other Macy's across the country. Downtown retail continued to struggle, and Pittsburgh's Macy's closed too. The historic Kaufmann's building was to be converted into condominiums, a hotel and street-level retail. Some of the Horne's branches in the suburban malls remained under the Macy's banner.

After its closure, loyal Horne's shoppers remembered the glory days when women put on hats and gloves to attend store events like this demonstration of Westinghouse appliances in the downtown flagship store.

Loyal Horne's customers recalled the glory days of downtown retail in Pittsburgh when women dressed in hats and gloves to go downtown and children put on their Sunday best to shop and then eat in the Horne's tearoom. Others remembered the excitement of new fashion, the glorious Symphony Gala and the sumptuous Bridal Salon.

It was a far cry from what has become twenty-first-century shopping: driving to a regional shopping center in whatever casual clothes are handy, stopping in a big-box store like Target or Costco or a "category killer" (named because of their ability to kill small-scale specialty retailers) like Home Depot or Office Max and then hitting a fast-food drive-thru for lunch. In fact, Walmart is the antithesis of the classic downtown department store with its no-frills décor, total self-service and mass distribution of low-price, low-quality general merchandise.

Cynics might say that it's no surprise that more and more people want to shop online from home in their pajamas.

Eating at Horne's

Horne's tearoom never acquired the popular following and cult status of its cross-town rival Kaufmann's Tic Toc Shop, where ex-customers still reminisced about its Mile High Ice Cream Pie years after its demise. Instead, it offered good plain food to weary shoppers and hungry businessmen and elegant luncheons to ladies in hats and gloves.

Restaurants were one of the earliest department store services. In the late nineteenth and early twentieth centuries, ordinary restaurants would not serve women unless they were accompanied by male escorts. Women would have to cut short a shopping expedition to return home to eat. Department stores recognized this and established tearooms, soda fountains and full-service restaurants. Women now had comfortable places to eat lunch or meet friends for tea.

Tearooms also benefited the store, although they were not generally profitable. After an elegant lunch, women could continue to shop. The cuisine was generally American, and the tearoom and other restaurant services were managed by a home economist.

It's not clear when Horne's first began serving food to its customers. By the early twentieth century, the store had a full-service restaurant on the sixth floor to offer "luncheon opportunities either to business men or to women on a shopping tour." In 1907, Horne's advertised a "Southern Luncheon" in its restaurant, and a December 1913 advertisement referenced a restaurant on the sixth floor and a tearoom on the main floor of the east building.

The original Horne's restaurant on the sixth floor, circa 1900; the restaurant was modest but provided a place for ladies to eat away from home.

In November 1915, it was advertising a "Special Football Luncheon," "guaranteed to put you in great spirits to root for your team." Lunch was served from 11:00 a.m. until 1:30 p.m. and quick service guaranteed so that diners could make the Pitt game. The special lunch featured Planked Sirloin Steak à la Horne and cost fifty cents.

A Horne's brochure at the time described "Our Restaurant": "When visiting Pittsburgh, and desiring a comfortable place to dine, our Restaurant situated on the Sixth Floor, will be recognized as a home like place. It is all of that and more; it is noted for its home cooking. Meals and lunches can be had at any time between 8:30 A.M. and 5:30 P.M. The charges are very moderate."

While Horne's added a new kitchen to the sixth floor in 1916, it appears that the restaurant closed in late 1915 or early 1916. It may have been replaced by the employee cafeteria, and food services for customers consolidated in the tearoom.

When Horne's expanded the store in 1922, it opened a tearoom restaurant under the balcony on the first floor on December 11, 1923. The new tearoom, which seated four hundred people, featured gray walls, brown mahogany woodwork and furniture and taupe carpet with black scrolls and small blue flowers. The windows were leaded glass with colored panels, and the curtains were gray. Peacock blue and orange hangings decorated the room. Reviewers found the new tearoom elegant.

The tearoom served salads, sandwiches, light meals and desserts. In 1929, "hundreds of women who are reducing by the Hollywood Diet" were "using the facilities of Horne's tearoom for their luncheons. All eighteen menus are served—so that you may have any of the luncheons on any day. A separate service station has been made in the kitchen to care for the requirements of this diet." The tearoom would also provide customers with a pamphlet describing the diet.

For those with heartier appetites, the tearoom served a Friday Special Lobster Lunch in April 1932. For sixty cents, shoppers were served a whole broiled Maine lobster, French fried potatoes, dressed lettuce, rolls and butter and a choice of beverage.

The tearoom also provided menu planning for entertaining and a "Hostess Buffet Service"—"Anything which is served in the tearoom you may serve in your home."

By 1937, Horne's had added a Soda Grill with a menu of fountain specialties like sodas, milkshakes and sundaes, as well as quick sandwiches. The grill appealed to those who didn't want to take the time for a longer lunch or who were on a budget. It was so popular with shoppers that it served 3,957 people on a single December Saturday night during the holiday rush. In 1940, the waitresses in the Soda Grill got new aquamarine uniforms that were "unusually spritely and pretty."

Horne's centralized its food buying and preparation so that the food served to employees in the cafeteria was the same quality as that served to customers in the tearoom and Soda Grill. In 1938, shoppers and employees consumed 1,500 turkeys in a single week. The bakery also provided products to the cafeteria, tearoom and Soda Grill. Employees there worked overnight to prepare products from beginning to end; Horne's baked goods were not made using factory production techniques. The store's baked goods were so popular with customers that Horne's opened a bake shop near the tearoom. The store also had its own in-house butchers to prepare its meat. The tearoom food was so well received that the restaurant was listed in *Gourmet Magazine* and in Duncan Hines's book *Adventures in Good Eating*.

When Horne's instituted its flood control measures after the devastating 1936 flood, it sealed its first-floor windows, including those in the tearoom.

Above: Horne's baked goods served in its restaurants were so popular that an in-store bake shop was set up outside the tearoom.

Opposite, top: In 1937, Horne's added a Soda Grill for those on a budget or who didn't want to take the time for a longer lunch.

Opposite, bottom: The Soda Grill served fountain drinks, as well as milkshakes, sundaes and sandwiches. It was wildly popular.

The windows were replaced with large photographic murals that would change with the seasons. On December 30, 1936, the employee Christmas Party was held in the "beautiful new Tea Room."

Menus from the tearoom dating from the 1950s provide a glimpse of standard tearoom fare. Horne's served a chicken salad sandwich, cream cheese and fresh pineapple on nut bread, a double-decker BLT, chopped egg and olive sandwich and jellied fruit salad with an assortment of tea sandwiches. Shoppers could order Melba peaches filled with frozen fruit salad and topped with whipped cream with butterscotch rolls. For "Afternoon Teas," there were waffles and syrup, assorted tea sandwiches or a hot ham sandwich with fried potatoes. "Cinema Suppers" included chicken à la king,

When store flood control was upgraded in 1937, windows in the tearoom were removed. The new tearoom was redecorated with wall murals. White linens and real china ensured an elegant dining experience.

steak and roast turkey with an appetizer, dessert and beverage; prices ranged from $1.20 to $1.70. The tearoom also served barbecued chipped ham on a bun and "Reymer's Blend." All menus from this era included a "Business Man's Special."

Often there was a featured lunch that tied in with a local event or merchandizing theme in the store. Menu cover art also reflected a theme and changed regularly. For November 1954, the theme was a "Foreign Fair" luncheon, and the country featured was Germany. The lunch of roast pork loin with potato dumplings, gravy, caraway sauerkraut, dark rye rolls and German apple cake (total cost: $1.30) was probably not that foreign to many ethnic Pittsburghers.

Some of the offerings seem odd to us today. In 1960, the featured lunch, "A Bit of Mexico," included "tacos" that were described as pancakes filled with pork. They were served with cauliflower guacamole and flan for dessert.

Other lunches included a "Vegetable Plate" with macaroni and cheese, bacon, spinach, lettuce and tomato; a cold salad plate with potato, chicken

This Christmas menu cover for Horne's tearoom may have been used in the store's centennial year, 1949.

and jellied fruit salad; tuna fish salad in a ring of tomato aspic; a tomato stuffed with crab meat and jumbo shrimp; and a green salad topped with asparagus and hard-cooked egg. The menu listed a full range of desserts: strawberry shortcake, apple pie, a pecan ball with hot butterscotch sauce and crème de menthe parfait. For those counting calories, the dessert menu helpfully noted "Individualized Saccharine Service Available Upon Request." Saccharine in coffee or tea instead of sugar would apparently allow a shopper to indulge in dessert.

Menu covers featured original art that celebrated local events. A menu recognized the opening of Gateway Center, another in 1959 Pittsburgh's bicentennial. Holiday menu covers changed from year to year; a 1959 menu cover illustrated holiday customs from the earliest days of Pittsburgh's history.

Department store tearooms were often the first place that children ate in public. One young Horne's visitor who was treated to lunch there remembered "starched napkins and tablecloths—china plates and cups and saucers—fine silverware—it really was an opportunity for a parent to teach their children 'manners' and 'table etiquette.' One spoke in hushed tones—sat up straight—and showed politeness."

Horne's welcomed its young tearoom visitors with special lunches for them and menus of their own. In March 1938, Disney's *Snow White* was so popular that it ran for an additional week at Loew's Penn Avenue Theater. Horne's advertised a "Festive Luncheon inspired by Snow White's cooking for the Seven Dwarfs." Parents were advised to bring their children to the tearoom before or after the movie for the special lunch.

Children's menus from the 1950s offer a glimpse into kiddie cuisine of the time. There were no pizzas, chicken fingers, hot dogs or soft drinks. Children were expected to enjoy adult food, although it was often rebranded to attract them. A Davy Crockett menu, illustrated with colored drawings of Davy, told kids that Davy Crockett often ate "Chopped 'Bear' Steak" (hamburger steak) on a corn sandwich bun with a "Frontier Salad" and "Coonskin Cap" sundae. In a Hansel and Gretel–themed menu, children were advised, "At the Gingerbread House Hansel and Gretel ate" creamed chipped beef and noodles, molded fruit salad, roll and butter, fresh strawberry sundae, milk or hot chocolate.

While the menus included colorful illustrations and a game to play, the food was adult: creamed chicken on mashed potatoes, hot fresh vegetables, fruit salad with an animal roll, sandwiches of cream cheese and jelly, chopped egg on whole wheat or ham. The store did offer a peanut butter sandwich, but children had to choose between peanut butter or jam. The beverage choices were generally milk or juice, although the store listed "cambric tea" for children, an old-fashioned drink of hot tea diluted with plenty of milk. While cake and ice cream did appear on the children's menu, other desserts were more wholesome: baked custard, jellied fruit or a fruit cup.

Horne's tearoom was not only a place for customers to lunch. It was often the scene of special events, especially during the holidays. Informal fashion shows were routine. In August 1937, Horne's advertised "Tomorrow… the Air-Conditioned Tea Room will be the scene of the most interesting parade of College Fashions you've seen!" During a Men's Fashion Show on a spring Monday morning in 1955, the tearoom served coffee and doughnuts to the men who attended.

In January 1967, Horne's proclaimed, "The most royal of highnesses King Friday XIII who rules over Misterrogers' Neighborhood of make-believe will observe his birthday on Friday the 13th and all of you are invited to come to Horne's Tea Room, Saturday morning…and celebrate a 'Happy Birthday' party."

By 1971, both the Easter Bunny and Santa were making regular holiday appearances in the tearoom. For a series of breakfasts before Easter, the bunny was bringing Chef Brockett, Mr. McFeely and the Horne's Sunny Bunnies with him. On the menu: Sunny Bunny Orange Juice, a big Nest Doughnut and hot chocolate. The breakfasts were geared to children, but they had to be accompanied by an adult.

In 1975, Santa also brought along Don Brockett, who staged a "mini-musical review" with Santa; Mr. Music, Johnny Costa; and the Horne's Holly Dollys. Santa was apparently as fond of sugar as the Easter Bunny, as breakfast included orange juice, a "Jimmy Horne" (described as "a pastry with a ton of chocolate jimmies on it"), hot chocolate, a candy cane and Froot Loops® with milk. The breakfast was described as Santa's favorite.

Mr. Rogers and Lady Aberlin also visited the tearoom—without a holiday celebrity—to autograph Mr. Rogers's book, *Mr. Rogers Talks About*. There was no information given about his favorite breakfast.

By the late 1970s, the Horne's tearoom was becoming less of a traditional tearoom and more like a typical restaurant. It began advertising dinners for shoppers who were encouraged to eat before staying to shop; the store was now open evenings several times a week and for special sales. It featured a holiday buffet as well as individualized service, perhaps as a way to cut costs. An "all you can eat" buffet in fall of 1976 provided hungry shoppers with roast beef, fried chicken, potatoes and ham au gratin, cold meats and cheeses, relishes and a variety of salad. The cost with coffee or tea and a choice of Horne's pastry: $3.50. In 1978, the tearoom was advertising Sunday buffets since the store was now open on Sunday for shopping.

On March 26, 1979, Horne's closed its tearoom, replacing it with a restaurant called Josephine's, which opened in August. The new restaurant, which seated 238 people, was described as a dining room broken into separate rooms. The largest section was designed as an outdoor New Orleans café with globe lamps, a fountain, wrought-iron tables and chairs and hanging plants. A large oak-stained wooden bar on a raised platform seated 85. Customers could enter the new restaurant from the Horne's store or from Stanwix Street. The street entrance meant that the restaurant could open on Sundays or after hours when the store was closed.

By June 1980, Josephine's was described in a review as "a very attractive restaurant with a Western saloon ambiance." The restaurant was calling itself Josephine's Eating and Drinking Emporium and featured a huge menu with large portions. All entrées included French fries and the "super salad table," a salad bar that included iceberg lettuce, beets, relishes, cottage cheese and choice of three dressings. Entrées described included quiche Lorraine and a variety of crêpes. The reviewer noted the reasonable prices and then commented, "Go to Josephine's when you're hungry and you'll be well served, but don't expect gourmet ecstasy."

Horne's merchandising tie-ins continued in the early days of Josephine's. In May 1981, the restaurant included a daily special from *Betty Groff's Country Goodness Cookbook*, as part of a "You've Got a Friend in Pennsylvania at Horne's" week in the store. The restaurant also set up a Josephine's Country Kitchen in the store's special events center, where they served a soup and a snack from the cookbook. Mrs. Groff gave a cooking demonstration and autographed her book in the store.

Ironically, Josephine's outlasted Horne's, continuing as a standalone restaurant after the store closed and eventually becoming Max and Erma's in 2004.

Minding the Store

The members of Horne's three founding families were very much active employees of the store as well as its managers, and they influenced its culture over the decades. Founder Joseph Horne set the tone for the following generations. Contemporary associates said that he conducted his business in a quiet way and, while interested in business, found time to participate in the philanthropic and religious movements of the day. Others noted that all of the store's founders "were church men and took great interest in church affairs." A *Pittsburgh Commercial* article from December 1867 commented, "Individually the members of the firm occupy the most credible social standing in the community." The three founding members—Joseph Horne, C.B. Shea and A.P. Burchfield—worked at the store until they died or retired.

The relationship between the three founders extended beyond business. Joseph Horne had married Mary Elizabeth Shea, C.B.'s sister, so C.B. Shea was his brother-in-law and uncle to his three children, Susan, Joseph and Durbin. When Mary died in 1863, Joseph Horne married her widowed sister, Emma Galloway. They had one son, Bernard Shea Horne.

Joseph Horne first lived on Penn Avenue near the corner of Galveston and moved in 1870 to Bidwell Street in Allegheny. He was one of the founders of the Christ Methodist Episcopal Church on Penn Avenue in Pittsburgh in 1852 and continued to support the church after it, too, moved to Allegheny.

At Joseph Horne's death, a Pittsburgh newspaper commented that he was "one of the pillars of Christ Methodist Episcopal Church" (now Calvary on

Pittsburgh's North Side). When he died, he was chair of the trustees for the church, which was building an edifice to replace the former church in the city, destroyed by fire. Joseph Horne did not live to see the new church. (His partner C.B. Shea had also donated $62,000 for its construction.)

Before his death, Joseph Horne and the other congregants had hired a young artist, Louis Comfort Tiffany, to design the stained-glass windows for the new church, paying him $15,770 to create 189 windows. With this commission, Tiffany perfected his technique of folding glass to create a layered effect, called drapery glass. When the new church was opened in 1895, its sanctuary featured three of the largest Tiffany windows in the world, each thirty feet tall. The Ascension Window was dedicated to Joseph Horne and the Resurrection Window to his partner C.B. Shea. (Visitors still come to the church to see its Tiffany windows.)

Joseph Horne was buried at Allegheny Cemetery, with the oldest store employees serving as his pallbearers. He left four children: daughter Susan and sons Durbin, Joseph and Bernard. Durbin succeeded him as president of the store. As part of the settlement of his estate, the wholesale business was sold so his descendants could focus on their retail business.

Durbin Horne served as president until illness forced his retirement six months before his death on May 13, 1916, his thirty-fourth wedding anniversary. Durbin was born on July 15, 1854. He got his education in the Pittsburgh public schools and at the city's Newell Academy before leaving for Hopkins Grammar School in New Haven, Connecticut, and then Yale. He graduated in the Yale class of 1876. After graduation, he spent some time at the Centennial Exhibition in Philadelphia before starting to work at the store. His father believed that men were handicapped without a fundamental knowledge of business that was learned from the bottom up. Despite his pedigree, Durbin Horne started at the bottom of the ladder; company history doesn't say if he worked as a cash boy. In six years, he had worked his way up during stints across the store and was made a Horne's partner in 1882. With the exception of his time at Yale, he lived in Pittsburgh, and the local press noted at the time of his death that he was "one of the best business 'boosters' this city has ever had." He was an active member of the Christ Methodist Episcopal Church, served on several bank boards and was a trustee of Carnegie Institute. His friends, business associates and store employees remembered him as a generous man.

Albert Horne, Durbin's uncle, was a popular store fixture, working until he was eighty-eight and never thinking of retiring. He died in 1935 after a cold turned into fatal pneumonia. He loved to share his memories of the

Left: Durbin Horne, son of Joseph Horne and his first wife, Mary Elizabeth Shea, succeeded his father as president of Horne's.

Right: Alfred Horne joined the store in 1865 just before the end of the Civil War. As keeper of the early store history, he died in 1935 at age eighty-eight after a short illness. He was still working at Horne's when he died.

early days of the store. During the seventieth anniversary of Horne's, he was asked his formula for a long life: "Serve the Lord—serve Him well—for that begets a vital, cheerful spirit and a vigorous mind and body." Then he apparently smiled at the interviewer and said, "Eating three square meals a day helps too."

Durbin Horne's younger brother Bernard spent his career as the store's general superintendent, retiring to a farm in New Jersey at age forty-five after twenty years at Horne's.

J.B. Shea, son of founder C.B. Shea, became president of Horne's in 1915. He didn't start his career at the store—after graduating from Princeton, he started out in iron and steel. In 1887, he joined the Pittsburgh Dry Goods Company, the wholesale side of Horne's, eventually becoming its president. When the wholesale business was sold following the death of Joseph Horne, J.B. Shea moved to the retail side. He left the store for the supply branch of the ordnance department during World War I but returned when the war was over. Like other Horne's managers, he was, as the press eulogized, "not only a great merchant, but a public spirited citizen." Ill health forced him to resign as store president in the summer of 1929.

A.H. Burchfield, son of founder A.P. Burchfield, was one of the most popular Horne's presidents. A brilliant merchandiser, he guided the store through the Depression.

Mr. Shea was followed by one of the most popular presidents in Horne's history, Albert Horne (A.H.) Burchfield, son of founder A.P. Burchfield. Born in Allegheny, Pennsylvania, he began officially working in the wholesale division of the company as an eighteen-year-old stock boy, although he had helped out during summer vacations from Allegheny public schools and Trinity Hall Military School in Washington, Pennsylvania. After three years, he moved to the retail side of Horne's.

Although A.H. Burchfield later took a business college course in Pittsburgh, he credited his early training to the three founders of the company: his father, A.P. Burchfield; C.B. Shea; and Joseph Horne. He worked at different departments across the store and directed merchandising for twenty years. Co-workers remembered that he kept the vital information about each store department on a series of four-by-six-inch cards that were always close at hand. He frequently ate lunch at his desk and was an incessant cigar smoker, often lighting a new cigar with the burning embers of the last one.

Mr. Burchfield was active in national professional organizations for retailers and in the Pittsburgh business community. He worked to improve flood control, particularly after the 1936 flood, and developed an early traffic plan for the city that would have used a system of subways and streetcars to ease traffic congestion. Failing health forced him to resign as president in 1939.

What endeared A.H. Burchfield to the other Horne's employees was his active support of Camp Horne. He and his wife lived at the camp during the summers, and he was an enthusiastic participant in camp activities. Horne's employees designated him as "Camper No. 1."

Following his brother's resignation, W.H. Burchfield became president of Horne's in 1939 and served throughout World War II. A 1902 graduate of Princeton, he became the store manager in 1907, and like his brother, he was active in Pittsburgh business and civic affairs.

By the late 1940s, the third generation of the founding families was working at Horne's. C.B. Shea retired in 1943 as vice-president and secretary, Bernard S. Horne was a director and general superintendent and Joseph G. Horne managed the glass and china department.

Durbin Horne's son Joseph had joined the store in 1911 after graduating from Yale. He started, like other family members, at the bottom, becoming a clerk in the adjustment department. Later, he worked in delivery and as a store buyer. He left Horne's to serve in the military during both World War I and World War II. He became a vice-president in 1929 and then president from 1946 to 1948. Joseph Horne died suddenly of a heart attack in 1948. Unmarried, he had no children.

A.H. Burchfield was also an active supporter of Camp Horne. He and his wife lived at the camp during the summers.

A.H. Burchfield Jr. was the last descendant of the original founders to serve as president of Horne's, following Joseph Horne's death in 1948. After graduating from Princeton in 1925, he joined the store in 1926, working his way up as a salesman and buyer before becoming general manager in 1946. Under his leadership, Horne's expanded into the suburbs, although he would remain an active booster of the city. He suffered a heart attack in his office in October 1961 and died one month later.

There were no fourth-generation family members available to assume leadership of the store. W.H. Burchfield's only son, Thomas, a senior at Pitt's law school, had been killed in a car accident in September 1961 while driving to the family's summer house in New York. But A.H. Burchfield had two daughters, and one of them had married a man who had joined the store. Richard Pivirotto followed his father-in-law as president of Horne's in 1961. He had married Mary P. Burchfield while still at Princeton. After graduating in 1952, he went to Harvard Business School, served for two years in the army and joined Horne's in 1956. During his presidency, Horne's became part of Associated Dry Goods, and Mr. Pivirotto moved to New York to become an executive with Horne's parent company. None of the presidents who followed him had any direct family link to the store.

"The Best Place to Work After All"

Many Pittsburghers considered Horne's a shopping mecca. For others, it was a great place to work. Like other downtown department stores, Horne's provided steady employment ranging from part-time and seasonal jobs for students to career-level retail positions. At a time when professional jobs for women were rare, retail provided opportunities in buying, marketing and advertising and management. Services in the stores—hair salons, alterations, restaurants—offered additional employment for women. Horne's also provided solid careers for men, some of whom joined the company as cash boys and rose to prominence as buyers or department heads. The store was proud of the number of longtime employees in its ranks; almost every year, several joined the Fifty Year Club.

In the nineteenth century, department store clerking was not a prestigious job. Prestige was reserved for the owners and elite buyers of merchandise like imported silks. Pay was low and working conditions grueling. Clerks worked long hours on their feet in stores that weren't well ventilated or air conditioned in summer.

In the early days, there was often a gulf between the backgrounds of working-class clerks and middle- or upper-class shoppers. Clerks needed to appear respectable and needed good social skills to sell merchandise. Speech was often an issue before mass communication; a clerk's speech might immediately identify her as a working-class girl. Department stores set up training departments not only to teach retail skills but also to refine the social skills of clerks.

From the earliest days, department stores provided training for employees. Here women are taught how to use a new color-matching system.

Class differences became less of an issue when department stores began recruiting women from middle-class backgrounds after World War I, and by the Depression, college girls were happy to find work in department stores. Men dominated store management in the nineteenth and early twentieth centuries, and some departments—furniture, rugs and bedding—remained male bastions until after World War II. But the twentieth-century fashion revolution was a boon to women. Men may have been fine selling fabric to women who would have dressmakers as fashion authorities. But as ready-made women's clothing became more popular, women clerks were often more adept at providing fashion advice to their women customers.

While women found career opportunities in department stores, there was less opportunity for minorities. Black workers were usually behind the scenes

Horne's store clerks, circa 1910. While all of them are wearing the popular shirtwaists and have their hair up in an adult style, it is clear that some of them were quite young.

doing drudge work and rarely appeared on the sales floor until the labor shortages during World War II.

By the early twentieth century, conditions had improved because of public outcry, and stores began providing employee benefits in response to public pressure. Some benefits were individual and offered relatively privately. A woman who joined the store before 1892 as a girl who wasn't even old enough to wear her hair up remembered that Joseph Horne was worried that she looked frail. He had a chair put in her department so that she could sit down. She stayed at the store for the rest of her life.

In 1910, Horne's established a salary and bonus plan for employees in selling departments. By the 1920s, the store was offering an array of employee benefits, summarized in a small booklet written by a young woman. The booklet, *Why I Like to Work at Horne's*, was first written as an article in the employee newsletter the *Horne-Pipe*.

The writer starts by addressing the prejudice against department store work: "You have heard girls say, 'Oh, I wouldn't have them to know I worked in a department store for anything.' But after all they are only the girls who have false standards of life and living, no doubt the same girls who judge another girl's character by the amount of rouge she uses and her 'boy friend' by the cut of his coat and the line of the pompadour he effects."

She continued by describing the workplace: "There is such a solid, substantial 'old family' feeling; such an assurance that one is working for a firm that is synonymous with good character and high ideals. The good stocks, the simple but impressive fittings throughout the store, the character of the people with whom one works....Our store is a leader in the great many philanthropical ideas—schemes which are intended to better our working conditions, and make things agreeable and pleasant for us."

She then listed specific benefits. Horne's was the first department store in Pittsburgh to shorten working hours by changing the closing time from 6:00 p.m. to 5:30 p.m. and providing a summer half holiday on Saturday. Unlike other stores that stayed open until 9:00 p.m. at Christmas, Horne's closed at 6:00 p.m.

Horne's was also the first store in the city to pay bonuses to both selling and non-selling staff, the first to allow staff to work reduced hours when sick and the first to advance salaries according to an employee's sales record for the year. After a year of service, employees received paid vacations. During World War I, forty employees in the service were kept on the payroll, and their families received a monthly check. After the war, they were welcomed back to their old jobs. They presented the company managers with a formal thank-you testimonial in 1920.

Employees could eat in a modern cafeteria with white porcelain fixtures trimmed in nickel. The food was ordered and cooked by the same staff who ran the store dining room and was offered at prices at or near cost. Employees could fill a tray and carry it to one of the tables or, for an extra charge, get served at the counter or at a table.

A Rest Room near the cafeteria included a Victrola, a piano and enough room to dance either at lunch or during "Goodfellowship Nights." The space could hold seven hundred people. There was a Conference Room with magazines, which was also used for employee training; a Smoking Room for men, also with magazines and newspapers; a Roof Garden; and a Promenade on the roof for those who wanted to exercise outdoors. After exercise, employees could use the shower room with its white tile, gray marble and shiny nickel fittings.

For those employees who were ill, Horne's had a nurse on hand for treatment and advice. The medical department included a large room set up with hospital beds and a treatment room. The floors in both rooms were covered in Oriental rugs.

The writer mentioned the social opportunities that the store offered—dances, a store chorus and the summer activities at Camp Horne. She also

Food served in the employee cafeteria was the same quality as in the restaurants and was prepared by the same staff.

mentioned the continuity of management—the sons of the founders were still running the business, and fifty heads and assistants of departments had been with the store for twenty-five years. About half of those had come to Horne's as young people. She concluded, "As someone has said, one should consider it a privilege to work at Horne's, because of the refined atmosphere we work in, and the fact that we are working with keen executives whose instruction is such that one has to pay large tuition sums to gain in schools and universities. Our daily experience here is valuable to us because Horne's schooling is recognized throughout the country as thorough, efficient training."

Benefits were expanded in the following years. In 1930, the medical service had a doctor and chiropodist as well as the nurse. A "welfare visitor" called if employees were sick at home or if there was a death in the family. A "sick allowance" was paid to ill or bereaved employees.

In 1931, a smoking room for women was added near the cafeteria. Between 1939 and 1949, Horne's established a Formal Pension Plan for employees and a Group Life Insurance Plan; costs for both were paid by the store. At some point, Horne's reduced the workweek to five and a half days and paid employees on legal holidays. But the perk that employees may have most appreciated was their employee discount.

In addition to the employee training that was provided on site, employees had access to courses at the Research Bureau for Retail Training that were given at Carnegie Tech and to special professional courses. For example, Mrs. Ella Baxter from the corset department was able to attend the Camp School for Surgical Corsetry. She was already filling doctor's prescriptions for special corsets for patients, and the store thought it important for her to increase her skills.

In 1941, the employee cafeteria was remodeled with a complete soda fountain like the downstairs Soda Grill for shoppers. It was open for lunch and then stayed open for the afternoon so that employees could stop by for a soda or milkshake instead of having to go to the crowded Soda Grill.

Employees were expected to look and act professionally. Most stores had strict dress codes, including Horne's. "Customers will trust your judgment if you dress appropriately for business," a code for women from the late 1930s or early 1940s stated. At that time, they were expected to wear suits or dresses with hems below mid-calf, along with tailored blouses. Basic dresses that could be worn with scarves or simple jewelry were recommended. Dresses were to have sleeves to the elbow; no cap sleeves were allowed, and sleeveless dresses weren't even mentioned. Suits and dresses were to be navy, gray or brown; prints were discouraged. Comfortable, well-fitting shoes "with a heel height that will not change your smile to a frown" were also recommended. Stocking seams were to be straight and slips out of view. Women were also advised to have clean hair in a simple style and well-manicured hands. They were to brush their shoes, remove spots from their clothing and avoid shoes with run-over heels. "When you know your selling appearance is right—you forget SELF—you concentrate on your customer."

A dress code from 1954 for men warned, "Blue jeans, loud sport shirts and shaggy hair may be 'real cool' in some circles but not at the Joseph Horne Co." Men were to wear jackets with shirts and ties, trousers and polished shoes. Many of them stuck with the ubiquitous dark suit.

There were also codes of behavior. One from the early twentieth century warned that employees were not allowed to eat or chew gum on the selling floor or use the telephone. There was to be no gambling during working hours and no drinking or coming to work drunk. All packages carried into or out of the store were to be inspected.

Clerks like this woman, assisting a shopper with gloves, had to adhere to a strict dress code.

Mention department store work and most people think of a girl clerk behind a counter. But department stores provided lots of opportunities beyond clerking. There were the buyers who selected merchandise, the people in the marking and receiving department who unloaded merchandise and tagged it before it was sent to the floor, bookkeepers and clerks, delivery drivers and warehouse staff and the people who provided services like tailoring, dressmaking and alterations. Food services, beauty salons, barbershops and interior decorating all required staff. Many department stores, Horne's included, manufactured or customized their own awnings, curtains, rugs and furniture so they employed crafts people. They ran a print shop.

In the nineteenth century, most stores hired children as young as twelve, many of them to work as "cash boys." At the time, there were no cashiers in the store's individual departments; a central cashier handled all of the money. Clerks would take payment for merchandise and hand it to a cash boy, or girl, who would take the payment to the central cashier and return with any change. Cash boys also ran other errands at the store as needed.

From its earliest days as a fashion arbiter, Horne's employed dressmakers and seamstresses. These women worked in tailoring and alterations.

With increasing pressure to eliminate child labor, cash boys were eventually replaced by pneumatic tubes—Horne's was the first store in Pittsburgh to implement the technology. But working as a cash boy was less oppressive than working in one of Pittsburgh's industries. Its glass factories, for example, employed armies of young boys. For many, a job as a cash boy was the foot in the door for a retail career. Every year, the *Horne-Pipe* recognized the new members of the Fifty Year Club. During the 1920s and 1930s, those employees had often started as cash boys.

Carl Goettman started working as a cash boy at age eleven in Horne's Library Hall store. He became a salesman in the men's furnishings department and led the department in sales. A natty dresser, he began voluntarily arranging the display cases in his department. When new merchandise came into the store, he would jump into the display windows himself and arrange the merchandise rather than waiting for the window dressers to do it for him. When the head of the display department retired, he applied for the job and was promoted. "Success...was instant and meteoric," the *Horne-Pipe* noted.

His windows, including Horne's famous bridal windows of the 1920s, were nationally known, and his sudden death in 1937 was a real loss to the store.

E.N. Lietman also started his Horne's career as a cash boy in the Library Hall store; he was fourteen. He remembered that the cash boys wrapped packages, ran errands and relieved other employees during their lunches, including the time keeper and floorman. He became a wagon boy later on one of Horne's two delivery wagons. Mr. Lietman rose through different departments at the store and held various jobs as stock boy, assistant department head and buyer before becoming a Horne's interior decorator.

They weren't the only cash boys to make good. Hugh Cunningham started working during his summer vacation in July 1893 and never went back to school. From cash boy, he rose to mail order boy and then office boy for store manager Elisha Holcombe. After working different jobs across the store, he landed in the mechanical department as a manager.

Louis P. Hoetzlein began as a cash boy in 1896. Later, he worked as the office boy for Durbin Horne for $2.00 per week. (At the time, wrappers were making $1.25 per week.) He became the office boy for the general manager and then for the chairman of the board. A.H. Burchfield bought him his first pair of long pants when he worked for him. Mr. Hoetzlein moved into the interior decorating department, where he worked for forty years decorating houses in Pittsburgh; Washington, D.C.; New York; and Watch Hill, Rhode Island.

Credit Manager Howard Leonard also began as a cash boy, starting in April 1894. He moved into the credit department, where he became a "memory authorizer"; in 1954, he could still remember the credit card rating on most of the credit card accounts. He had interviewed more than 200,000 customers seeking Horne's credit and became the store's first sixty-year employee.

Another cash boy became a wrapper and then worked in the bookkeeping department before beginning to make signs using rubber stamps. Durbin Horne sent him to art school to improve his sign-making skills. Another cash boy became a wrapper and then worked at the warehouse filling pillows and bed ticks with feathers. He began selling brass hardware and rose to become an assistant drapery buyer. Durbin Horne sent him to New York to get merchandising ideas and told him to be sure to take a recreational side trip up the Hudson River while he was there.

One former cash boy remembered what work was like. They and the wrappers didn't register their time on the regular time clock. Instead, at lunchtime, a timekeeper recorded how much time they took for lunch.

The cash boys had their own separate lunchroom, as they did not eat with the clerks. The room had a long table in the center with a bench on either side. Lockers without doors lined both sides of the room. Boys would put their lunches in the lockers only to find later that they sometimes had been moved.

The man remembered that the wrappers kept stubs for every package they wrapped and at the end of the day dropped all of the stubs in a box by the elevators, where they were taken to the auditing department. As mail orders were filled by clerks for the mail order department, boys took them to a desk under the stairs on the first floor. Two other boys were in charge of the desk and would take the packages to the mail order department, where they would be shipped.

Young people didn't only begin their retail careers as cash boys. One man went directly to the marking and receiving department, where he spent his entire fifty-year career, watching the department grow from five people to seventy. Another man, J.F. McCleery, who became the manager of the receiving department, started in October 1888 as a wrapper in the Library Hall store. After six months, he said that the work was "too light" so he was moved to the receiving department, which had only three employees at the time. There were no elevators in the store and no delivery trucks. Since the store handled dry goods, much of the merchandise that it received was huge bolts of linens and dress goods. The men carried the bolts on their shoulders—perfect work for a boy who thought wrapping packages wasn't hard enough. Later, the department was expanded when it was also made responsible for marking goods with prices.

Mr. McCleery remembered that there were no set employee hours; people in the department stayed until the work of the day was done. In 1935, he took over as manager of Camp Horne, a "temporary" position that continued until the camp was closed at the beginning of World War II. He continued to manage the receiving and marking department, where one hundred people handled all merchandise from the time it was received from suppliers until it moved to the floors of the store.

Not all of the cash boys were boys. Young girls were employed in department stores too, although more often as wrappers. Mary Agnes McCully, fourteen, put up her hair to mark her grown-up status and walked in to ask Joseph Horne for a job in the 1880s. He hired her as a cash girl. Her first job was running cash and hanging stock. She eventually worked in the women's clothing department, where clothes were custom-made for customers, who spent hours getting fitted.

She rose through the ranks to become a buyer and was sent to New York on buying trips. "See those!" she later told a Pittsburgh reporter. She pointed to her feet in sturdy, square-toed shoes. "When I went on buying trips in the good old days I'd wear out a couple of pairs, just like that. None of the dressmaking houses—even the very elegant ones where they carried all of the Parisian imports—had elevators and they were spread from one end of New York to the other. Oh, I tell you we worked in those old days."

Not all employees joined Horne's as young people. R.G.S. Ruffner relocated from Indiana, Pennsylvania, in 1894 to work as a silk salesman, a relatively prestigious job. He remembered that dress silks were a huge part of Horne's business and that plaids were in style. Each salesman was expected to know the clan tartans by name. Selling silk was a high art, and he remembered that there was no formal training for new employees. They were given a sales book and told to go to work. He realized that lack of training was a problem and later, with more experience at the store, always took the time to train the new employees in the department.

Ruffner also told the *Horne-Pipe* writer about one of his treasures: a time clock key. In the late 1890s, each employee was given a large key with a number on it. They would insert the key in the time clock, and the clock would print the number on the time card. After Horne's burned to a shell in 1897, he searched the debris after the fire and found a time clock key. When he looked at the number, it was his own key, no. 232. He experienced another fire in 1900 and three floods and rose from silk salesman to Horne's service superintendent.

M.S. Thompson joined Horne's delivery department in 1896 as driver of one of the delivery wagons and spent his entire career there. He received a salary of ten dollars per week. In 1903, he drove the first motor delivery truck to appear on Pittsburgh's streets, a Conrad two-cylinder steamer. He remembered how noisy it was. Horne's continued to use horse-drawn wagons for delivery because many of the city's roads were in too bad shape for motorized trucks. Mr. Thompson helped A.H. Burchfield select the location for the future Camp Horne and transported equipment and people to the camp. When he retired, the single truck he had first driven had grown to a fleet of one hundred vehicles.

For some employees, working at Horne's became a family tradition. "My father worked at Horne's. He started in the retail business in 1923," a retired employee told a reporter in the 1990s. The employee himself had started at the store at age seventeen, two days after graduating from high school. His first job was as a "locker boy." "When somebody showed up at work without the key to their locker, I opened it for them." By the time he retired, he had worked his way up to purchasing director.

John Nawojski, who was working at Horne's when it closed in 1994, was the fourth generation to work there. His great-grandmother worked at the store in 1898 as an interpreter. She was a well-educated Italian immigrant who spoke four languages, according to an article in a Pittsburgh newspaper:

The first floor of Horne's had millinery, yard goods, ribbons, that sort of thing. Wealthy women from the North Side would send their servants to Horne's to buy bolts of cloth, but most of the servants couldn't speak English. My great-grandmother would listen to them and translate it to the salesgirls. She was a very successful woman. She got into a donnybrook with my great-grandfather, who was a conductor on a streetcar, because she made more money than he. She was paid $13 for a 60-hour work week. In those days, Horne's was open every night so that mill workers could shop after work.

His grandmother worked at the store in 1917 and 1918. "Her greatest memories were the war bond rallies that Horne's used to have. She got an autograph from Mary Pickford during one. She said the day armistice was declared, the store was closed and there was a big party for all the employees. They had food from the restaurants." His mother wrapped packages and did stock work during two summer vacations in 1937 and 1938.

Dorothy Helmstadter started at Horne's in the beginning of the Depression. She was well educated, with an undergraduate degree from Ohio Wesleyan College and a master's degree in English from Harvard, as the article continued:

I was in middle management, in charge of the junior employees. Junior employees were all of the people then called wrappers, people at the cashier's desk who wrapped packages, and also stock boys. In those days, wrappers would put your purchases in whatever was convenient for you to carry. If you wanted it gift-wrapped, there was no charge, of course. And there was free delivery to the suburbs too.

It was at the depth of the Great Depression, or the height, or whatever you want to call it. I was very happy to get a job at Horne's after finishing at Harvard. [All of her female colleagues in middle management were well educated.] *Oh, there was someone who graduated from Vassar, another friend from Wellesley, one from the University of Michigan—*

we were all college graduates. These were the glory days. It must sound incredible to you, but Horne's really took such good care of its employees.... For instance, the junior employees all got a free week's vacation at Camp Horne down the Ohio River. Any other employees could vacation there, for $12.50 a week, which included breakfast and dinner and sleeping in a tent. It was so much fun. Horne's had all of the amenities for its employees. There was a full time registered nurse, and I was in charge of a library for employees. There were about 3,000 employees then.

We were paid well then for our work. I recall very vividly what I was paid because I thought it was quite high—$1,800 a year. The junior employees under me were paid $12 a week. We all worked a six-day week. During the Christmas preseason, the wrappers would work overtime and get extra money, as well as 50 cents supper money, which was a big boon to them. If an employee found a misspelling in a Horne's ad, you got a dollar. They were always very, very dignified ads then. Everything was dignified at Horne's. If you were in the management group, the executive group, you had

Horne's offered many opportunities beyond clerking. These men and women may be processing payments in their basement workspace.

*to wear navy dresses. And nobody was on a first-name basis at Horne's.
Everyone was referred to by their proper title, Mr. Mrs., or Miss.*

*A member of the Horne family, Mr. Albert Horne, who was in his 70s,
was at the store every morning. He worse striped trousers and a cutaway
coat and a bright red tie—very formal attire. He would stroll through the
store every morning, a very distinguished-looking gentleman with snow-
white hair. Then he would sit in his open office and read the newspaper and
take another stroll through the store. Horne's was known as the store with
the carriage trade. The doorman at Horne's was a real tradition. When
I was there, he was a very tall, impressive-looking black man ushering
everyone in. He was such a well-known person in Pittsburgh.*

Jane Vandermade, who retired as fashion director in 1992, started working
at Horne's in 1947. "If you got a job at a good company, you stayed there."
She began as an assistant in the fashion office and became fashion director
in 1960. During the 1960s, "no one in the fashion office was without hat
and gloves. And, of course, no one walked around town in sneakers and
sweatsuits. It was a different world....I just consider myself lucky because I
had a wonderful career at Horne's, at a wonderful time of retailing."

As fashion director, Ms. Vandermade was renowned for Horne's annual
Symphony Gala, according to an article in a Pittsburgh newspaper on the
occasion of Ms. Vandermade's retirement:

*We had the first Symphony Gala in 1965 at the Carnegie Music Hall and
we sold out—700 tickets....We decided to put on two shows, and the last
few years we had three shows with 5,000 to 7,000 attending. We used
a professional lighting and sound man, and a designer and set designer. It
was very professionally done. I used to do the choreography and pick out
the music. The gala was always in September, and I would put it out of
my mind through Christmas, and start thinking about it again, and start
working on it in March, after I got back from the collections in Europe....
It was our 25th year in 1989, and we stopped and thought, how long can
this go on. The whole world had changed, and we decided to move on to
something else. We felt it was right. Actually, we spent as much money the
next year for another benefit for the arts.*

John Nawojski, a fourth-generation employee, started his Horne's career
in 1977 as a clerk in the basement budget shops called the Gateway Shops.
"In 1987, when they closed the Gateway Shops, I came upstairs, to the first

Opportunities for black Americans were often limited in department stores. While Horne's had a black doorman, others usually worked behind the scenes, like this man recycling cardboard circa 1940.

floor in men's furnishings. Actually, my whole family ended up working on the first floor." He was working at the store on its last day. "The joke is, my great-grandmother started when the plaster was drying and I'm leaving when the plaster is falling."

Minorities usually didn't get the same opportunities at department stores as their white counterparts. Horne's did hire black Americans, and they appear in department photos in the *Horne-Pipe* from its inception in the early 1920s. Minority employees did not ascend to store management; they usually worked in store maintenance, in manufacturing and as porters.

Horne's hired one of its first black employees in 1865, ex-slave Robert Tocas. He came to Pittsburgh as an eleven-year-old and worked as a cabin steward on steamboats that traveled between New Orleans and Pittsburgh. At thirty, he became a porter at Horne's when it was still located on Market Street and handled all store deliveries using a wheelbarrow. He later worked on a delivery wagon and, shortly before his retirement in 1919, on the store's cleaning crew. He named one of his six children after store president Durbin

Horne. Horne's was proud of Mr. Tocas and his long tenure at the store and used his image with his delivery wheelbarrow in its centennial celebration.

By the last half of the twentieth century, minorities were becoming more prominent at the front of the store, as they were hired in management and as sales staff. In 1977, Arnold Zegarelli hired Alfred Dean as Horne's hair salon's first black stylist. As Zegarelli said later in Mr. Dean's obituary, "I learned from Deano to be color blind. Deano taught us that hair is hair. It doesn't matter if it's on a black or a white woman." Mr. Dean became popular with co-workers and customers for his elegant sense of style; he wore perfectly tailored suits in all colors, and his shoes were always shined. He was also able to impress with his technical skills and reportedly dazzled his co-workers with his ability to wield a curling iron.

Horne's wasn't only a place to work. There were opportunities for play. Over the years, the store employees could join together to bowl, play tennis, swim or play baseball. As early as 1919, they could attend a gym class held in the seventh-floor Roof Garden.

Many of the men in the store belonged to the Men's Club, first organized in 1907 or 1908; longtime member Albert Horne wasn't sure of the exact date. The five-hundred-member club held regular meetings with speakers and entertainment, as well as an anniversary dinner in the spring and a banquet each fall. Events were held in Horne's tearoom, and roast turkey was often on the banquet menus. In 1907, banquet entertainment included a minstrel show; it was put on by employees, none of whom appeared in blackface. At a meeting in the early 1930s, when the economy was in trouble, store manager W.H. Friesel spoke on "The Gold Standard and Currency Inflation." At a 1935 meeting, the club held a less serious checkers tournament. In 1949, "Muzak" replaced the live dinner music at the banquet.

Banquet
TO
The Association of Men Employees
OF THE
Joseph Horne Co.
WEDNESDAY, APRIL 3, 1907
S.C.8,

Men who worked at Horne's had opportunities for entertainment, including annual banquets.

Employees also held regular dances. An announcement for the February 1930 Washington Birthday Dance declared, "No games or side issues, just dancing to the hotsy-totsy, heated melodies of 'Viv' Sandek and his Knickerbocker Boys."

To raise money for the Employee Outing Association, which organized summer entertainment, particularly for the "junior employees," Horne's employees held an annual follies. These were serious productions staged off site at the Syria Mosque or a theater. The Second Annual Minstrel and Follies in the fall of 1923 included many store employees, some performing in a popular Floradora Sextette. Six girls wore lace and feathers and large Floradora picture hats, while six other girls with slicked-back bobbed hair were their boy escorts. An article on the follies in the *Horne-Pipe* commented that the chairman of the Show Committee had eaten cheese sandwiches for dinner for a month while he stayed late and worked on the show.

Other talented Horne's employees could join the men's chorus, the girl's chorus or the mixed chorus. The mixed chorus had one hundred members and was led by a paid director. The chorus, one of only two permanent department store choruses in the country, was the brainchild of A.H. Burchfield and was established in 1926. By December 1930, the chorus was singing carols from the store balcony at 9:00 a.m. each morning and broadcasting an expanded Christmas musical program on WJAS during the week. Its performances got rave reviews in the local press.

Sometimes the store entertainment was outside. Betsy McHugh remembered working in Horne's advertising department on the afternoon of October 13, 1960, during the World Series when Bill Mazeroski hit his epic home run. The advertising staff was watching the game on a TV in the department, according to a Pittsburgh newspaper article on the game:

> *When the home run was hit, I, along with everyone else in the department rushed to the fourth floor windows to see everything that was not tied down raining onto Stanwix Street. Computer cards floated from office windows like leaves falling from trees. I stripped the fourth-floor ladies room of toilet paper, hurled it out the window and watched it slowly flutter and zig-zag into the street below. People hung out of windows and waved to other people, total strangers hanging out of office windows across the street. Car horns blew in never ending bleeps and blares, and everyone yelled and yelled and yelled.*

But it was the store picnics that led to the most employee fun. Annual summer picnics apparently began in 1897, when the store still employed young teenagers as cash boys and wrappers. The Fifth Annual Picnic was held at Kennywood Park on July 12, 1902, on the "Saturday Half Holiday." The picnic committee invited Durbin Horne, A.P. Burchfield, A.H.

Burchfield and J.B. Shea. There were races for the twenty-five cash boys and five wrappers who attended: the Cash Boys 50 Yard Dash, the Wrappers 100 Yard Dash, a Potato Race, a Three-Legged Race and a Sack Race. They had a greased pig contest, a greased pole contest and a costume class called a "Burlesque," as well as a baseball game. This may have been a "Basket Picnic," where employees brought their lunches in baskets on the day of the picnic and the baskets were transported to the picnic grounds. There was free coffee for those who had brought a "receptacle" to drink it from.

The Twelfth Annual Picnic was held at Rock Point Park on July 17, 1909. The store closed at 1:00 p.m. that Saturday; there was a band concert at the store from 12:30 p.m. until closing. Employees could bring their picnic baskets to the store or buy food at the park; baskets were sent along with them on the train. There was another band concert at the park and dancing in the evening.

While picnics at local parks were popular, store managers decided that they needed a more permanent venue for employee recreation. They began looking for land and found a likely parcel on the wooded hills above the Ohio River not far from the Emsworth train station in 1907. Future picnics would be held at Camp Horne.

A model of the early store was featured at Horne's Picnic of the Century, held at Camp Horne in 1949.

The last employee activity was bittersweet: a reunion of former employees on September 14, 1997, at the Rose Barn in North Park. By then, even the Horne's survivors who had worked at Lazarus were former Horne's employees. Five hundred people attended from around the country, including two past presidents, Robert O'Connell and Michael Pulte. The Rose Barn was decorated with a paper-and-cloth replica of the famous Horne's Christmas tree that appeared on the corner of the store every holiday. Inside, various shopping bags from the collection of two forty-four-year employees showed the evolution of the Horne's logo. Store employees shared their memories, with most agreeing that Horne's was the best place to work after all.

Horne's for the Holidays

Holiday celebrations were big events for department stores; in some
ways, they transcended the opportunity to tie merchandising to
the calendar. They could be just plain fun.

For consumers in the early twentieth century, Halloween was a major
holiday usually celebrated at home. In October 1915, Horne's advertised
everything needed for a home Halloween party, including corn poppers,
sauce pans and molds for making candy, taffy pans, nut bowls, decorations
and children's novelties like squeakers, masks and lanterns. To add to the
festivities and make cleanup easier, there were paper table covers, napkins
and plates.

Spring openings, timed for Easter, were also big events. They were
popular in Pittsburgh into the 1920s, even though they had been abandoned
by department stores in more progressive cities. In March 1914, an
advertisement for Horne's in the *Pittsburgh Press* declared, "Pittsburgh's
Easter Millinery as Decreed by Paris," and went on to provide details on the
newest styles, much like a fashion article. The advertisement included a list
of the hats available from leading French designers, including Paul Poirot
and Jeanne Lanvin.

The spring opening, where customers could find the newest spring
fashions in time for the Easter Parade, evolved into general Easter
celebrations. At Horne's, these included an annual marionette show that
started in the 1920s and continued for more than a decade. The show had
a different theme each year, often involving Peter Rabbit. The store also

SANTA
Still at Work
GIFT SHOP
AND
TOY STORE
Open Monday

This little boy is patiently waiting for Santa to arrive at Horne's. Christmas was the most important holiday for department stores.

held annual breakfasts with the Easter Bunny for children. These endured even after the Horne's tearoom had been replaced with Josephine's. A live Easter Bunny also appeared in the children's department much like Santa Claus. With the bunny was an Easter Egg Plant with giant crystallized eggs as fruit and a rabbit artist who painted eggs. Horne's also sold Easter eggs in its candy department. Once shoppers had decided on a size (up to five pounds) and a flavor (coconut and fruit and nut were popular), the store would pipe on the name of the recipient at no cost.

But from the very beginning, the biggest holiday of all was Christmas. The first reference to Christmas at Horne's was an article that appeared in a local commercial newspaper in December 1867. There is no mention of Santa or reindeer or toys. The article, which reads more like an advertisement, just noted discreetly, "as the Holidays are near at hand it will not be inappropriate for us to give our readers an inside view of this extensive concern." The article listed all of the available goods department by department. Anyone receiving a Horne's Christmas gift was assured of something practical—gloves, lace, fabric, trimmings for a hat.

By the time Horne's moved to Library Hall, Christmas was a bigger event. A similar article, published in 1872, called Horne's "A Fairy Home of Fancy Goods" and said, "Christmas will soon crown the year." "That fairy home of holiday goods—the retail headquarters of Messrs. Joseph Horne & Co., which are now overflowing with the evidence of preparation for the festival season….We can…advise our friends that nowhere else will they find more courteous treatment or find such a place to purchase holiday goods." Again, the presents would be practical. The expanded Library Hall store sold not only fabric and trimmings but also men's clothing and accessories and some women's clothing.

By the late nineteenth century, Christmas was the major holiday for department stores around the country. Stores began displaying elaborate Christmas windows and incorporating Santa into their imagery. Across town, upstart Kaufmann's was running large, graphic Christmas ads. Horne's, by contrast, simply presented "Plain Facts for Holiday Buyers" in 1889. Those plain facts included the ease of shopping at the store, still located in Library Hall: "Aisles all cleared of center counters. Extra help behind the counters. Your only inconvenience will be the crowds of buyers. You won't mind that. You come here because everybody else does. Room for all. Every preparation for the final grand Christmas rush, in the stores and out. Perfect arrangements for hourly delivery of goods…in any part of the two cities." The promises were followed by a long list of goods in the best dry goods tradition. While Horne's had added some silver, it still wasn't selling toys. Any children receiving a Horne's Christmas gift would be getting clothing or the fabric for a new suit.

By 1907, Santa had found his way to Horne's, where he appeared in the store's toy department. He didn't arrive in print like Kaufmann's Santa in a large ship from the North Pole. Instead, Horne's provided a brief reminder that the store was open at night up to and including December 24, as well as that the restaurant served dinners until 9:30 p.m. "You might also make a note, for the benefit of the tots of your family," the announcement stated coolly, "that SANTA CLAUS IN PERSON IS A FEATURE OF THE TOY DEPARTMENT."

By 1913, Santa was arriving in the store in late November to officially open the toy department for the Christmas season. Toys had become big business, and Horne's toy buyer was traveling to Leipzig and the Black Forest in Germany every summer to find toys for Christmas. In a Horne's ad for the event, a jolly Santa in a red suit was seen opening a large crate of toys for children. That Saturday, the display of new Christmas toys was formally unveiled: a running electric railway, climbing monkeys, a hobby horse on wheels, Japanese tea sets and imported paints in a tin box.

In the early days, Santa was not a permanent fixture of the toy department, so Santa's few Saturday visits were special events. As Horne's explained in 1915, "Santa Claus Here Again Saturday. We had expected that we could induce him to spend but one day with us. So many children missed him last Saturday and so many have expressed a desire to see him, that we have induced him to visit us once more before Christmas." Apparently, thousands of children had visited Santa the previous Saturday and had received a gift. Toys on sale included a bisque-headed doll with sleeping eyes for $1.75, a mechanical train set for $2.50, imported Teddy bears with jointed limbs for $2.50 and eighteen lithographed picture blocks for $0.18. The new Tinker Toys building sets were also on sale that year.

But for parents who didn't want to indulge children with too many toys, Horne's had some advice. In a December 1915 ad, the store noted, "Clothes head the list of practical gifts for boys."

Santa didn't only reign in the toy department. By 1915, Horne's was calling itself "the complete Christmas store...'The Best Place to Shop

In the 1920s, Santa arrived at Horne's on a decorated float as part of Pittsburgh's "Santa Parade."

for Christmas.'" It was a place that generations of department store holiday shoppers would recognize: "Christmas trims throughout the store. Christmas merchandise displayed everywhere." The advertisement was also an appeal for customers to do their shopping early, noting that while traditional Christmas shopping started after Thanksgiving, the year 1915 was an exception, although it didn't explain why. Early shoppers would have the best opportunity to buy choice merchandise in comfort.

Horne's also advertised practical gifts for adults. A large ad for "Wear Ever" aluminum in 1915 recommended that men consider the new cookware as a gift for wives. "We have had considerable experience with women and are sure that, in the great majority of cases, such a gift as this will appeal to them as something out of the ordinary." In addition to individual pieces, men could buy complete sets for wives: twenty pieces for $20.00; six for $7.00; fourteen for $12.50; and seventeen for $18.00. The gift suggestion also revealed something about Horne's shoppers: more and more women were doing at least some of their own cooking instead of relying on servants. The store also hosted demonstrations of the latest Westinghouse electrical household appliances; waffle makers, coffee percolators and toasters were popular, practical gifts.

For those who didn't want to shop or were confused about what to buy, they could consult the store's "Gift Granny." An ad for the service on December 4, 1919, advised shoppers, "Simply bring the list of those to whom you wish to give Christmas gifts—as many names as you please—to Gift Granny in her Chimney Corner here." Gift Granny would then write to each person on the list and ask for gift suggestions, including size and color. Gift Granny would not reveal the name of the person who had consulted her, adding a "touch of mystery," and the service was free. Shoppers were reminded that it took several days for Gift Granny to write to the gift recipients and receive an answer back, so they should "consult her without delay." While the name of the Gift Granny service would change over the years, it would remain an annual Horne's Christmas service.

The popular after-Christmas sale also debuted at Horne's in the early twentieth century. An advertisement in 1912 thanked customers for shopping at the store, making it their best Christmas season in their history, and advised them that the sale would begin the next day, December 26.

With the economic prosperity of the 1920s, Christmas continued as a major event on store calendars. At Horne's, planning for Christmas 1922 began in June because it had become so complex, encompassing interior and exterior decorating, merchandise and decoration of the store windows.

For 1929, store décor reflected religious significance, with purple for the Three Kings and gold for the gifts they brought. At the two Penn Avenue entrances, miniature replicas of the Westminster Abbey were displayed. Horne's had them specially made by a Belgian woodworker who had traveled to London to copy them.

A newspaper article in November 1924 described the trip of an imaginary mother and two young children into the city to visit Pittsburgh's department stores. While other stores included elaborate mechanical scenes—brownies helping Santa in his workshop and Christmas with the Katzenjammer Kids—Horne's windows were rather staid. There was lots of merchandise on display—Oriental rugs, women's clothing, clocks, men's top coats and evening dress. For the children, there was an entire window of dolls—"mamma and papa dolls and little baby dolls and little girl and boy dolls."

Dolls were also featured in an advertisement for the toy department that told parents, "Even the little ones who frighten at elevators can be brought safely to the Horne Toy Store without getting a chance to scream, for the Toy Store here is conveniently located in the Basement, just a few steps down. The stairs are right inside the Main Floor entrances so that it is not necessary to take the children on crowded elevators, or through the store." In addition to dolls, the store was selling Buddy L trucks for boys.

The economic prosperity of the 1920s couldn't last; department store historian Vicki Howard has commented that the Depression hit Pittsburgh particularly hard. Holiday sales in the city dropped 23 percent in 1932. By 1931, Horne's training department was staging an "Anti-Depression Skit" for employees to get them into the holiday spirit. W.H. Burchfield, vice-president of the store, was one of the players.

Still, the Horne's holiday advertisements give little indication that their customers might be struggling economically. They are filled with the traditional high-end gifts that the store had always carried—perfume, furs and women's and men's evening wear. Santa continued to visit the store, and his visits lasted longer. In 1938, Horne's Santa spoke to an entire group of schoolchildren about the North Pole and asked one little girl to put out water for the reindeer. The store Santa at the time was popular Sandy McGregor, who returned to the store year after year. He also delighted children by putting the well-known Stanwix Street cop over his knee and spanking him. The cop had been pestering Santa.

In the 1930s, the Horne's Chorus was regularly singing Christmas carols from the store balcony and, by 1938, broadcasting carols on radio station WWSW in fifteen-minute segments.

World War II dominated Christmas during the early 1940s. A Horne's advertisement in December 1941 showed Santa in a jeep with GIs as his helpers. During the planning for Christmas 1942, someone on the planning team suggested:

> *This year we should be concerned with making our Christmas campaign a matter of restraint and good taste. The public, I believe, will resent a jolly "same as last year's" Christmas. It's about time retailers took the war seriously. Some of the public even now resent full warehouses and business as usual. It could be worse by Christmas. Let's build good will for the store this year by recognizing the war and the people's efforts, help to guide them in wise buying habits and get back to first principles and tell them what Christmas should mean. Build up their good will.*
>
> *Headline Ideas: The Hope of the Future; Welcome the City's Newcomers into Your Home This Christmas (for those uprooted and forced to move to Pgh for defense work), Working This Christmas ("A salute to local defense workers, many of whom will be working on Christmas Day."), The Third Freedom "Christmas is a religious festival. We are fighting for religious liberty, one of the four freedoms." An ad that would advance our prestige. This is what Christmas should mean in war time. If we had the courage to do this ad, feel we would be contributing to a better, more wholesome Christmas, and the good will engendered would reflect in our sales.*

Among the themes suggested for advertising: "If It's from Home, It's from Horne's"; "Duffel Stuffers; Make Sure This Continues—Buy Another War Bond"; and "Present with a Future—Children with War Bonds."

A woman who worked in the display department wrote to her manager, "My second suggestion had to do with the wrapping and delivery of packages. I have heard customers criticize the waste of unnecessary materials in wrapping and I'm sure they would be glad to cooperate in any plan to save." Soon Horne's was recycling and reusing cardboard and other packing materials.

In 1942, the retail merchants in Pittsburgh sponsored a Toy Parade on Saturday, November 21. The parade passed three sides of Horne's, and when it was over, Santa, still played by Sandy McGregor, appeared on his Candy Cane Throne.

Gifts for sale at Horne's included war bonds and bookends and ash trays made from the "blitzed stones of London." The carved stones were decorated with a symbolic English medallion, and a portion of each sale was donated to the RAF benevolent fund.

This Christmas window from the 1940s used a storybook theme, complete with Raggedy Ann and Andy.

By 1943, Horne's and other department stores had trouble finding the additional holiday help that they relied on each year. The government's request to conserve electricity was a challenge to the display department. At Horne's, silver leaves were used to decorate the Street Floor columns instead of the traditional lights. But by 1945, Horne's advertised, "Our entire store is ready for a joyous post war Christmas."

In 1946, Horne's held a special Men's Night Before Christmas, when men could shop for women on their list. Women could fill out a Gift Hint Card in the store, and the store would send it to the men so they could buy the gifts their wives, daughters and girlfriends really wanted. There was also a Stag Shop, an annual area where men could shop by themselves without being distracted by women.

Special annual holiday shops for women included a *Vogue* Gift Shop, with accessories chosen by fashion staff at the magazine, and The Christmas Box, a shop with gifts from different departments throughout the store.

Horne's now had a new Santa—Sandy McGregor had retired—who greeted children from a Gingerbread House in the toy department. One year, the corner Christmas window included storybook characters like Pinocchio, Puss in Boots and Little Red Riding Hood. Other windows featured Victorian figures, told the story of "The Night Before Christmas" and included a toy village, where a boy lay sleeping surrounded by animated toy figures.

Horne's also sponsored holiday programming on local radio, including a Christmas drama featuring Betty and Bob and a fantasy character named Cloudchaser. Letters to Santa from local children were also read on the show.

And Gift Granny had evolved into a team of Santa's Helpers, who wore red-and-green costumes designed by Edith Stewart, head of fashion at Horne's, and made in the store. The helpers would make suggestions to uninspired shoppers or shop for all of the gifts on a customer's list. One helper assembled 650 individually chosen gifts for schoolchildren. Another escorted a child who couldn't walk to see Santa.

Holiday exuberance dominated Christmas in the late 1940s, as shoppers were finally able to buy merchandise that had been unavailable. It continued into the 1950s and 1960s with the postwar baby boom.

In 1950, a new character joined Santa at Horne's: Christopher Candycane. Apparently, the idea behind his creation was to have a non-Santa character to promote the toy department.

As a brochure titled "The Story of My Life" explained:

> Long ago, Aunt Samantha Snowball, who is Santa's cook, ran out of flavoring and coloring just when she had one more Christmas candy cane to make. Santa suggested that she use the juice of the magic fir tree for flavoring and a holly berry for coloring, since all of the North Pole Super Markets were closed. She did. But from this unusual recipe, instead of a candy cane, a live impish, lovable elf came into being. He said that his name was Christopher Candycane and that the antenna springing up from his cap was magic radar. "With it you can tune in on people's thoughts…anywhere in the world." And when he touches his radar, whatever he wishes comes true. Of course, Christopher Candycane never goes anywhere at Christmas-time except to Horne's in Pittsburgh.

In 1950, Christopher Candycane invited children to the Horne's holiday party in the tearoom and, in 1951, toured Pittsburgh with a dinosaur from Carnegie Museum of Natural History and was featured on the tearoom menu.

Soon, Christopher Candycane was appearing with Santa in advertisements and in Santa's toy department realm. He reached the high point of his Christmas activity in 1957, editing a special issue of the *Horne-Pipe* and appearing on radio with a special song, in twenty-second TV spots and in the Christmas windows. In one window, Christopher was carrying tools, a ladder and paint. The explanatory sign read, "I'm

Inside the store, Horne's included Christmas figures as part of the décor that reflected an annual theme. This Victorian family decorating their tree may have been used during the store's centennial Christmas in 1949.

Working on a Corner Window Which Shows the Life and Times of Christopher Candy Cane [*sic*]." The corner window featured toys and a special song along with Christopher.

The same year, a real person in costume in the toy department appeared as Christopher Candycane along with Santa. For some reason, never specified, the live Christopher was less than successful. In 1958, a member of the special events staff noted, "I will suggest in my 'report' that we do not have a Christopher Candycane, but a clown attendant for Santa. There were so many complaints last year about our Christopher that we had better not repeat unless we can find a very small masculine 'actor.'"

Christopher was more successful as a merchandising device. Horne's sold scarves, pins, barrettes, bracelets, dolls, puzzles, polo shirts and aprons with Christopher Candycane's likeness on them, a total of $3,785 worth of

This Horne's window from the 1950s celebrates the birth of Christopher Candycane, with Santa and his cook presiding.

merchandise. It added additional items the second year, and a Christopher Candycane candle was so popular that it was sold for several years.

Christopher Candycane had quietly faded from view by the end of the 1950s, but not Santa. Horne's took its presentation of Santa seriously, developing guidelines and holding training for its store Santas. (There were now Santas in the branch stores as well as downtown.) It didn't allow pictures with Santa and didn't sell photos with Santa, like some stores did. The number one rule for Santa: "Never promise anything definitely to a child...if a child doesn't get the present that is promised him, he may experience a shock."

In a letter to a professional colleague, a member of the event planning staff shared other guidelines for Horne's Santa. Santa referred to himself as "Santa" not "I"; he didn't preach to children; and instead of telling them to eat their green beans, he suggested that they try them. When children asked for dogs and parents were unwilling, Santa was to say, "When you are a lot bigger and can take care of a puppy yourself of course you can have one."

Sometimes the store Santa would talk to all of the children in a family at once; when he did that, children tended to ask for gifts for their siblings rather than for themselves. Older children sometimes came to see Santa to ask for a gift that the parent had vetoed. School and Scout groups liked to sing to Santa, and he liked to join in. One day, two little deaf girls came to see Santa and couldn't read his lips because his beard was in the way. The Horne's Santa just held and rocked them while their mother cried.

One Santa talked to so many children that he lost his voice and had to take three days off. When he returned to work, Horne's sent him to the Mount Lebanon store, where he wouldn't have to talk to as many children as he did downtown.

When children came to see Santa at Horne's, they could leave a letter for him in a special mailbox. Children also wrote to Santa in care of the store. Parents also wrote. In one letter, the mother of a three-year-old explained that the little boy's father had died earlier in the year, and she was asking if Santa could encourage him to sleep in his own bed again and not with her. A note on the letter indicated that a reply had been sent.

In most cases, Horne's used a standard reply letter from Santa that changed from year to year. The letter was illustrated with Santa and Christopher Candycane. The letter's envelope did not use Horne's address as sender, but rather a picture of Santa, so that even the smallest children could recognize it. The letter from 1954 was typical:

DEAR LITTLE FRIEND

My what a thoughtful child you were
To write me that nice letter

Of all the joys at Christmas-time
There's nothing I like better

Than to hear from all my little friends
And to learn that they've been good

Even my reindeer liked your note
And they said that if they could

They'd like to write and tell you
That you make them happy, too.

But since they haven't learned to write
I'm sending this message to you.

My helper, Christopher Candycane
Is mailing this letter to you.

It brings my wish for your happiness
To last you the whole year through.

Your Friend Santa Claus

P.S. come to visit me in Horne's Big Toy Store, I'll be there until Christmas Eve

In 1957, Horne's started a new Christmas tradition: talking to Santa on the telephone. The toy department had opened for Christmas on November 9, and Santa was already ensconced there when Horne's announced that children could call the store on a December Friday night between 6:00 p.m. and 9:00 p.m. and talk to Santa Claus. All they had to do was dial "Court-one-three-ho-ho-ho" (CO1-3000)—Horne's telephone service number. Horne's had one hundred volunteer male employees on hand to answer the phones.

Two boys dressed as Davy Crockett, complete with guns, visit Santa in the 1950s.
Apparently, this Santa didn't think they would shoot their eyes out.

Horne's and Bell Telephone were not prepared for the response. The men answered between twelve thousand and fifteen thousand calls, and the telephone company's busy meter showed that an additional eighteen thousand calls were busy. Bell also estimated that thousands and thousands of other calls were simply uncompleted. The demand shut down the Pittsburgh telephone system and systems in surrounding districts. Bell and the U.S. Army demanded that the tradition be nipped in the bud; had there been a disaster in Pittsburgh, the area would not have been able to respond with the telephones tied up by Santa.

Meanwhile, the men answering the phones were busy. A *Horne-Pipe* article related their experiences as they talked to the children. Many of the children were clearly influenced by television advertising in what they asked Santa to bring. Others asked Santa for things he couldn't bring:

"Daddy to come back." Children asked for gifts for their family members, and one boy asked for a bone for his dog. Santa talked to multiple children on some calls. One call had eighteen children on hand to talk to Santa. When Santa asked one little girl if she had any brothers or sisters she told him, "No, but mommy is pregnance."

Some children told Santa that there would be cookies and milk waiting for him, and one little boy told Santa that he would leave out "a cold beer." After one child told Santa what treats to expect, his dad could be heard in the background saying, "And he better eat the d....stuff." Another dad told his child to ask Santa if he knew a good number to play.

One child who made a mistake in dialing got a downtown police station—its number was similar to Horne's. When a cop answered the phone, he heard wailing on the other end, "Santa's not in jail, is he?" The policeman had to reassure the child that no one in custody answered to the name Santa.

Following the "Santaphone Session," the volunteers headed to the Roosevelt Hotel for refreshments. While the volunteers had a good time and the event was a success for the store, it would not be repeated.

The next year, Horne's set up red-and-white "Magic Telephones" in the toy department, twelve in the downtown store and three in each of the branches. Bell Telephone set them up so that children would hear a taped message from Santa when they lifted the receiver. There were pauses in the one-minute tape so that children could respond to Santa. Children lined up by the dozens to talk to Santa on the magic phones without shutting down the Pittsburgh telephone system.

A report on Horne's Christmas activities in the toy department reveals its careful planning and philosophy about the holiday. While other stores installed their Santas early in the season, Horne's waited until after Thanksgiving for its Santa to appear. At the same time, it sponsored a local TV program featuring Santa that let the children know when he would be arriving from the North Pole.

Santa left the North Pole on November 27 and was scheduled to arrive at Horne's by boat on Friday, November 28. He arrived in the middle of the season's first big snowstorm, but thousands were on hand to greet him. The huge crowd followed Santa to the store, where they waited hours to talk to him. The Magic Telephone concept and Santa's arrival by boat were so popular that they were repeated for years.

By the 1950s, Horne's was also beginning to participate in citywide holiday events, beginning with Christmas at Gateway Center, the area across Stanwix Street that was being redeveloped with new office buildings and a

Horne's issued annual Christmas toy catalogues, like this one from the 1950s.

Hilton Hotel. The first Christmas program at Gateway in 1952 centered on a large tree, fifty-three and a half feet tall, from the wilds of Bradford Woods in the North Hills. The tree was decorated with 1,500 lights and 1,800 plastic-coated cardboard ornaments. It took two days to erect the tree and three days to decorate it. Horne's mixed chorus sang during the tree lighting program, and an angel, made by the Horne's display department, slid down a cable from the eighth floor of the Gateway Building and threw the switch to light the tree. The Gateway tree lighting became an annual event that featured choral groups from Pittsburgh industries and churches.

By the late 1950s, Horne's was broadcasting seasonal organ music from its Gateway music department. Amplifiers placed on top of the Gateway 2 building were connected to the department, where Joseph Deotto, an organist, played a five-minute program every two hours. The phenomenon of outdoor live music got lots of press coverage for Horne's and for Gateway.

While Horne's participated in public events, the store tried to ensure that the religious tone it took in the store translated into wider events. Planning notes for the late 1950s include ideas on how to keep the religious tone of Christmas in holiday events. In one memo, the Gateway event was called "Xmas at Gateway," and a Horne's manager crossed through "Xmas" and changed it to "Christmas."

Christmas was also celebrated in all of the Horne's suburban branch stores.

Horne's continued its own Christmas traditions inside the store. Planning for the holiday started in June. In 1955, the display department ordered one thousand yards of fabric to cover forty-nine columns, seven hundred yards of garland, three hundred bows, greens, seventeen large wreaths, six special trees and twenty-four figures. It took teams of people days and days to decorate the store.

There was a Stag Shop set up for men to shop without women and a Lilliput Gift Shop where children could shop while parents waited outside. A holiday gift shop, again aimed at men, was set up in Gateway 3 for businessmen.

For large items that might be difficult to deliver in time for Christmas, Horne's developed a special gift card. At the time of the sale, the clerk would take a Polaroid photo of the appliance or piece of furniture and insert it into the card. The card read, "Santa is bogged down," with the promise of after-Christmas delivery. Horne's also developed a small chart that shoppers could fill out with size information for those on their lists to help them remember what to buy.

By the 1950s, the Santa's Helpers had become Horne's Santa Belles. One woman reminisced on a department store website:

It took months and months for Horne's display staff to plan for Christmas. Here columns on the first floor are wrapped to look like candy canes and are complemented by festoons and elaborate trees.

I remember going Christmas shopping with my dad and sister. We always went to Horne's. Dad would take us up to the mezzanine where he would hire a Santa Belle. These were college women working over the Christmas season. My dad would tell them what he wanted to buy and the Santa Belle would take us to all the departments and help us select presents for my mother. We would eat lunch in the restaurant on the ground floor. When we were done shopping, the Santa Belle would take all of the packages back to her desk. She would arrange to have everything gift wrapped and shipped to my dad's office in the city. I don't know how much this service cost but it was great. The Santa Belle was allowed to get merchandise out of display cases so we didn't have to wait for a department sales clerk to help us.

While people shopped, Christmas chimes played at regular intervals, and the Horne's Chorus of one hundred voices sang carols every morning from 9:00 a.m. to 9:30 a.m. from the balcony. Carols were also broadcast on KDKA and by shortwave radio to Commander Byrd at the South Pole. Other groups sang in the store each evening from 5:00 p.m. to 6:00 p.m. On Christmas Eve, just before closing, there was a choral processional through the store, led each year by a different church choir.

Outside, the Christmas windows featured a different theme each year. In 1953, Santa watched while animated angels on clouds went about different holiday activities. Santa himself and his sidekick Christopher Candycane had their own windows.

In 1953, Horne's started its most beloved tradition: the giant illuminated Christmas tree on the corner of the store. The tree was eighty-five feet high and eighty feet across at its widest point; 4,500 lights on one and a half miles of wire formed the branches of the tree, which was anchored to the store by half a mile of steel cable. Thirty large illuminated ornaments decorated the tree's branches. The tree, which was lit from 5:00 p.m. to 1:00 a.m. each day, took almost 1,659 man-hours of labor to install. It was usually lit at a special ceremony inaugurating Horne's holiday season.

This Horne's Christmas window is themed "The Night Before Christmas."

Horne's continued its traditions into the 1960s. Santa arrived on the day after Thanksgiving on the Good Ship Lollipop of the Gateway Clipper Fleet. The ship was decorated, and a band on board played holiday music. At the time, Horne's Santa was KDKA's Ed Shauganessy. The boat would sail up the river, turn around and come back to the wharf, where another band would be waiting to escort Santa to the store with a parade. A bank of elevators at one of the Stanwix Street entrances, not normally used for customers, was decorated as a rocket ship to take shoppers directly to the seventh floor, where Santa held court.

One child remembered the elevators years later. "The outsides had rockets on either side of the doors and the inside of the car walls were lined with buttons, switches, and lights that you could play with as if you were in a rocket ship. The elevator operators were dressed as space men and they would do a count down before the elevator went up. They actually played rocket sounds over the inside speakers for effect. It was great."

Santa also arrived at the branch stores with a parade, by fire truck in Mount Lebanon and East Hills and on a parade float at Natrona Heights.

Horne's also continued its Stag Shop. In a comment posted on a department story history website, one woman who worked there in the 1960s remembered it:

Only men were allowed into the snug back room decorated in the style of an exclusive mens' only club with subdued colors, leather covered club chairs and heavy wood tables. The shop was filled with very nice items from sparkly jewelry to fur coats. The men were offered a glass of sherry along with a tray of Christmas cookies from the first floor bake shop. I was one of the college age girls who staffed the room. We ran around the store gathering a selection of items that the gentleman shopper suggested his wife might like. Sometimes, we were asked to model the item, be it a jacket, a dress or a negligee! The shop provided us girls a few weeks of work during Christmas break. It was wonderful to become familiar with all the departments in the store and get to know the other staff. I always felt fortunate to have been a part of the Stag Shop for two seasons.

By the 1970s, Horne's was continuing its most popular traditions, but it became more and more active in general downtown festivities like Light Up Night and in the charitable activities that KDKA organized for Children's Hospital. Santa's Magic Telephone evolved into Horne's Hot Line, where kids could talk to Santa from a Throne Booth. Conversations were recorded and

Announcements of new suburban stores were often a part of Horne's Christmas promotions. In 1951, Santa delivered a new store in Whitehall.

later played on KDKA. Santa presided over a Candy and Cookie Palace, where Candy Cane Girls helped him. The children's Secret Gift Shop continued, as did the Santa show on KDKA.

For grownups, relaxing with dinner after a day of shopping, different high school choirs from around the region sang from 6:00 p.m. to 7:00 p.m. in the tearoom.

In 1977, Santa was in his Castle downtown, where he was accompanied by a giant talking Raggedy Anne, seven feet tall. Children who came to see Santa could also leave a letter in the North Pole Mailbox. Choirs continued to sing during dinner in the tearoom. One of the store windows featured the work of Joan Webb, a Horne's artist who had created a "backyard fantasy" with a "merry band of creatures" called Hornswoggled. Horne's also sold her book in the book department. Horne's teamed with Pittsburgh Ballet Theater to promote its *Nutcracker*, and dancers visited the store in costume.

For teenagers who wanted something more modern, there was a Saturday disco with live music.

There was one Horne's tradition that the store did not follow throughout the 1970s. In 1978, the illuminated Christmas tree on the corner of the building was dark. The store was trying to conserve energy during the energy crisis.

Horne's partnership with Pittsburgh Ballet Theater continued into the 1980s, with dancers visiting South Hills Village and Monroeville Mall as well as downtown for mini-performances from the ballet. There was also an exhibit of costumes and props from other ballets, including the classics *La Sylphide* and *Swan Lake*. Horne's also designed and sold a commemorative poster to benefit the ballet. To benefit Children's Hospital, Horne's designed and sold a Christmas card that depicted the illuminated tree on the corner of the downtown store. It also developed and sold a commemorative limited-edition glass ball ornament decorated with the tree.

Santa Claus was back, but now Horne's was allowing photographs to be taken with him and selling them to parents for $3.50 each ($2.50 for each additional copy). In a seasonal gift shop run by the Pittsburgh History and Landmarks Foundation, shoppers could find unique pieces of historic memorabilia. Those with no time to shop could pick up prewrapped gifts at the "Wishes with Wings" shop downtown and at all of the suburban stores.

By the end of the 1980s, Horne's Christmas was permanently linked to Light Up Night. As part of the celebration in 1989, Franco Harris and L.C. Greenwood threw the switch that lit the tree for both Horne's and Fifth Avenue Place. Santa was in his Snow Forest, surrounded by animated creatures and the 3WS Talking Christmas Tree. Horne's Christmas activities were linked to the Pittsburgh Broadway Series and WQED. Caroling by the Horne's Chorus was replaced with caroling from the Pittsburgh Oratorio Society. Horne's was still selling its special edition Christmas cards featuring the store's corner tree. The perennial Breakfast with Santa got a twist with toy soldiers from the Civic Light Opera accompanying Santa. Breakfast—egg, bacon and cheese on a muffin, hash browns, orange juice and hot chocolate—was served in the Special Events Center, which had been transformed into Holiday Hall.

Personalities from KDKA continued to broadcast from one of Horne's windows and collect donations for Children's Hospital. Many of these traditions continued until Horne's permanently shut its doors on Christmas Eve 1995.

This Horne's Christmas catalogue for 1953 shows the iconic lighted tree on the corner of the building, a holiday tradition that outlived the store.

One tradition remained after Horne's downtown flagship store became a short-lived Lazarus and then headquarters for Blue Cross/Blue Shield: the massive corner tree. Lazarus erected and lit the tree for one year before turning it over to Blue Cross, the new tenant of the building. Blue Cross, now Highmark, has continued to set up the tree, a massive effort involving a crane and a large work crew, in time for Light Up Night.

The company gave the tree a new name, the "Unity Tree," but to most old-time Pittsburghers, it's still the Horne's Christmas Tree.

Playing at Camp Horne

While Horne's employees may have appreciated their company clubs, gym classes in the Roof Garden and a chance to sing in one of the company choruses, the real center of employee recreation, especially during the summer, was Camp Horne. Located in the hills above the Ohio River at Emsworth, about nine miles below the city, the camp was considered "a fully-equipped summer resort": "Camp Horne has one fundamental object—that of furnishing a place for recreation and enjoyment and a source of beneficial outdoor life for the employees of the Joseph Horne Co. store, and their friends."

The camp had humble roots. In the late nineteenth century, a group of women employees approached manager A.H. Burchfield about providing a treat for the "Junior Help." These youngest employees included the cash boys, messenger boys, delivery boys and the young girls who worked as wrappers and stock girls. At the time, boys could start working as age twelve, earning $1.50 to $2.00 per week.

The group, which was formally incorporated later into the Joseph Horne Company Employees' Outing Association, held its first picnic in 1898. After organizing picnics for several years, it opened a two-week camp in Valencia, Pennsylvania. The two-week camp was so successful that the company began to look for a spot in Allegheny County to rent or lease for a larger camp.

In 1907, it found the property in Emsworth. It took three years for the Outing Association to raise the money to rent the grounds for two months.

WHEN YOU'RE AWFULLY BLUE—
AND THERE'S NOTHING TO DO,
AND YOU FEEL FRIENDLESS
AND FORLORN.

TAKE MY TIP—IT'S A PIP—
JUST PACK UP YOUR GRIP,
AND RAMBLE DOWN TO
CAMP HORNE.

For employees, Camp Horne was a memorable perk of working at the store.

It made $400 from a big picnic held at Rock Point, $800 from a minstrel show held at Carnegie Music Hall and $1,500 from a winter carnival in the Exposition Hall. The balance came from small donations from employees and their friends and from contributions from the store managers.

The earliest camps were strictly for the junior help and were relatively basic. Children boarded the train in Pittsburgh on a Friday and rode to the Emsworth station, where they were met by a "bus," a "motor top" mounted on a wagon that was drawn by two of the company's white draft horses. The bus could carry twenty-two people at a time—uphill two miles onto a private road, across a ford of Lowrie's Run and then to the top of an open field. Spread below were twenty-five white tents set up in the fields. A lean-to stable had been constructed for the horses.

The only permanent building on the property was the kitchen. The children slept on cots in tents; each tent held six cots made up with linen sheets, woolen blankets and white spreads. A locomotive bell from the Pittsburgh and Lake Erie Railroad was rung to call them to meals. They washed their hands at a "bosh," a range of tin wash basins set up on a board outside the kitchen, and ate at tables set up outdoors under a canvas roof. Milk, cream, vegetables and meat were stored in a cool root cellar, and hearty food was prepared by a resident cook. The children were encouraged to eat as much as they liked. One little girl gained six pounds during a week at Camp Horne, and a boy gained ten pounds.

At night, the camp was lit by twelve large Weisbach gas lamps, each with six lights. Gas for the lights was piped 1,500 feet to camp. Gas light wasn't provided to the tents. Instead, each tent had a kerosene lantern, and the last camper in bed doused the lantern. Lights were expected to be put out by 10:00 p.m., and the rising bell was rung at 7:30 a.m.

The camp was managed by a woman who was also a trained nurse. In addition to the cook and kitchen staff, there was a day and a night watchman for security.

The children weren't even asked to make up their own cots but rather were encouraged to play outdoors. There were open fields for croquet and baseball. Lowrie's Run had been dammed to create a large artificial lake one thousand by one hundred feet and four feet deep, and there were swimming lessons for those who didn't know how to swim. The depth of the lake could be controlled by a series of boards, cement crocks and pulleys so that the water could be lowered enough to allow the smaller children to wade.

Two store employees, a man and a woman, organized the activities each week. Baseball teams from the store came to play at the camp. One afternoon, the managers and buyers played against the floorwalkers. On another afternoon, the elevator operators took on the floorwalker team.

Store managers supported Camp Horne and contributed money to buy the camp property. In this photo from the 1920s, Alfred Horne is third from the left in the first row and A.H. Burchfield is third from the right. The third man from the right in the back row is wearing the uniform of the store's baseball team.

Lowrie's Run had been dammed to create a lake for boating and swimming.

Entertainers came out from the city two evenings per week. A large tent was set up as an auditorium with an upright piano to provide music for dances and theatricals. The camp also had its own stationery that was given to children so that they could write home.

Adults from the store could come out to picnic for the day. While they couldn't eat in the dining tent with the children—there was only room under the tent for sixty campers—they could set up saw horses and planks under the trees. They had to bring their own food in baskets, but the camp would provide coffee, tea, lemonade and "the best spring water."

Not only did the employees in the Outing Association raise the money to establish and run the camp, but they also did much of the work at the beginning and end of the season, setting up and taking down the tents, maintaining the property and raising money and in-kind donations for equipment.

In its earliest days, Camp Horne operated as a retreat for the Junior Help, but changing labor laws soon prohibited child labor. By 1919, the camp had been converted to a camp for any employee who wanted to spend part of the summer in the country. The Outing Association continued to manage the camp and raise money for it. In October 1922, 3,500 attended a benefit dance held in the newly completed sixth floor of the store, which served as a temporary dance floor. The group also held a card party in November. In March 1924, the women organized a Leap Year Dance, a company first, to raise money for the camp. In November 1925, employees organized and presented the third annual Horne Follies at the Syria Mosque with 200 fellow employees in the cast and original songs and musical numbers. The public was encouraged to attend.

By the 1920s, a tent city had been erected in open fields at Camp Horne. *Courtesy of Avonworth Historical Society.*

The Outing Association rented or leased parcels of land before buying them and was slowly able to accumulate 125 acres of woods and open field. By the 1920s, most of the permanent and semi-permanent infrastructure was in place, and the camp became a center of summer activity for Horne's employees, opening in June and closing in September.

In December 1923, Allegheny County agreed to pave two miles of road below Ben Avon Heights Road and named the new paved portion Camp Horne Road when it was completed in spring 1924. With the new paved road, campers could drive out from the city and park in the lower portion of camp along Lowrie's Run. In 1925, a steel bridge was erected over the creek.

By 1927, the temporary tents set up in the field had evolved into rows of tents with wooden floors and double canvas roofs along a system of streets. Each tent contained an iron bed and a chiffarobe with drawers and space for hanging clothes. Tents were eventually supplied with electric lights. The tent city could house two hundred people.

There were tents for single men and women, tents for families and three tents for black employees, two for women and one for men. There were also separate washrooms for men and women, with hot and cold running water and showers. A permanent recreation pavilion had replaced the earlier tent, and there was a permanent dining hall not far from the kitchen that could seat two hundred. The recreation pavilion had one of the best dance floors in the area. Paved roads, walks and bridges connected the different areas of camp, and sewers and electric lights had been installed. In improving the camp, the association had retained the country charms that attracted them to the property in the first place: the brook, the shade trees and the acres of green grass.

Each year, the association upgraded camp. In 1919, two tennis courts, a running track and basketball and volleyball fields were added. In 1928, improvements included cement walkways and a radio receiving set, and in 1929, Horne's added a new merry-go-round and equipment for bocce. Three

Enjoy Life at

CAMP HORNE

Season
of
1927
Commencing June 25ᵗʰ

JOSEPH HORNE CO.
Employees' Outing Association

An annual program summarized camp rules, activities and charges and included a map of the camp. *Courtesy of Avonworth Historical Society.*

pay phones now allowed campers to make local and long-distance calls.

In 1928, the store also added four "magnificent new parlor car buses" to take employees back and forth from the store. Buses to camp left the loading platform on Duquesne Way behind the store every summer evening at 5:15 p.m. and returned to the store from camp every morning at 7:30 a.m. Horne's employees could also take the Emsworth streetcar to Plummer Avenue and walk the two miles through the town to the original upper entrance to camp. Those who took the train could be met at Emsworth Station by appointment. Those with cars could drive; the camp had limited garage space and lots of parking.

Employees could come to camp for the day or stay for a night, a weekend or a week. Families and guests could stay as well. Regular transportation into town allowed some employees to live at the camp for portions of the summer and go into the city to work.

The camp was run by a permanent summer staff that included a manager, cooks and kitchen staff, a nurse and staff who made up the campers' beds each day. For employees and members of their immediate families, costs for camp in 1928 were $1.25 per night, $2.75 for a weekend and $8.50 for a week. Other relatives and guests paid double the employee rate. Guests could stay for only three days in a given week, and children under one year of age were not allowed to stay overnight at camp. Camp charges included three meals a day, and day campers could make arrangements for meals only. A Corner Store sold refreshments, including desserts from the tearoom, and the kitchen would make up picnic baskets if they were ordered in advance.

Camp rules were minimal. Junior campers had to go to bed when the first bell was rung at 10:15 p.m., and all visitors had to leave camp at that time. Those staying overnight had to head for bed when the two lights at the swimming pool were turned out. There was to be absolute silence

Campers could board the "Tally Ho" at the Emsworth train station for a ride to Camp Horne. *Courtesy of Avonworth Historical Society.*

after taps was played at 11:30 p.m. so everyone could sleep. Meals had to be booked in advance, and employees had to get passes for their guests. In 1929, a new rule was added: "Running around the campus in bathing suits is absolutely forbidden."

Meals in the dining hall were prefaced with the official Camp Horne Blessing: "Be present at our table, Lord. Be here and everywhere adored. Thy creatures bless and grant that we may feast in Paradise with Thee."

In addition to the tents, the kitchen, the dining hall and the recreation pavilion, Camp Horne had permanent sports facilities. As one camp booklet declared, "It makes every Joseph Horne Co. employee a member of a select country club." There was "swimming in a modern sanitary pool" twenty-five by seventy-five feet, with a large slide and a swimming instructor on hand when the pool was open. There was a nine-hole miniature golf course and quoits, croquet, sockey ball, basketball and volleyball. There were fields for baseball. Employees could play tennis on "three of the finest gravel and grass courts in Western Pennsylvania" or hike on camp trails and surrounding country roads. The picnic grove was equipped with an outdoor oven, barbecues, tables, benches and swings. Tuesday night was "Athletic Night," where an athletic trainer led organized exercise. A different orchestra played almost every night in July at the dance pavilion and on every Thursday night in August, where "a good orchestra will play the snappy jazz music of the day." There was often dancing on Saturday nights as well. On Sunday

A large swimming pool supplemented the camp lake and was often used to stage special swimming and diving exhibitions. *Courtesy of Avonworth Historical Society.*

evenings, there were often movies—on one Sunday, it was the movie *Brotherly Love* and an *Our Gang* comedy.

Camp life wasn't all fun. In July 1930, fifty-five store employees led by camp manager J.W. McCreary and E.P. Shatz, assistant manager of Horne's, used shovels, a garden hose and wet sacks to fight a fire on a nearby property that threatened one of the camp buildings. After four hours, the building was saved.

Horne's began holding its annual employee picnics at Camp Horne. During the 1920s, these were called "basket picnics" because employees could pack their food in baskets and have the baskets transported to the camp. The picnics were usually on Saturday afternoons. The employees would check their baskets in at the store before they started work and receive a ticket for each basket. The baskets would be transported directly to camp. In the 1930s, the store cafeteria would make up picnic baskets for employees who ordered in advance. Cost for a basket ranged from twenty-five to fifty cents. Employees could take special streetcars from Stanwix Street to Emsworth. While the store provided free coffee, employees could buy soft drinks, ice cream and candy.

Horne's twenty-fourth annual picnic in 1921 was typical for the era. Employees worked in the morning, and the picnic was scheduled for their afternoon "half holiday." Once they arrived at camp by car, train or trolley,

After Camp Horne Road was paved in the early 1920s, Horne's employees could easily drive to the camp. A large parking lot accommodated private cars. *Courtesy of Avonworth Historical Society.*

there was a comedy baseball game, tennis matches, swimming and races for men, women, girls and boys. The feature of the day was the Fat Men's Race, where I.B. Campbell beat A.H. Burchfield and two other men to win a new corncob pipe. There was dancing at twilight and more dancing in the evening. Often, picnics included diving and swimming exhibitions. In 1929, Aileen Riggin, the "World Champion Girl Diver," was featured at the picnic.

One girl whose father worked at Horne's remembered, "Every year came the highlight…Picnic Day. Camp swarmed with employees and their families. Rides, races, tennis tournaments, and always a Spectacular at the pool. Famous swimmers like Gertrude Ederle who had just swum the English Channel, came to give exhibitions. And always, the greased pole event was hilarious."

The Men's Club also had a picnic, as described in a letter by a girl whose father worked at Horne's (the letter can be found in the Camp Horne file at the Detre Library):

They always had a day of races and games ending with a Treasure Hunt. Even though Dad had made up the clues and distributed them around the camp, I was allowed to enter the Children's Hunt. One year I got the clues mixed up and saw a prize at the bottom of the pool. I quickly changed into my bathing suit and dove in and came up with a bag of pennies…$5 *worth! Then I saw the tag and realized that it was the Men's Prize. By that time, some fellows were watching me and stretched out their hands for the prize…but I threw it back into the deep end of the pool, and five or six of the fellows dove in with their clothes on and thrashed around until one emerged victorious.*

Some Horne's families spent the entire summer at camp. The girl who found the pennies at the bottom of the pool was one of them. She remembered:

As soon as my sister, Beverly, was old enough, our family began spending the entire summer at Camp. The cost for the four of us was $34 per week (including meals). I used to get up for breakfast with Dad, after which he left to drive to work, and I carried a tray of food to Mother and Bev. Mothers filled their days with bridge games while we kids played. Once, after a hard rain, Mr. Burchfield organized all the kids into a work crew (foreman and all) and paid us a dime an hour to dig drains at the sides of the paths and fill them with stones. Kept a bunch of kids out of trouble for awhile….We would pick wild strawberries and blueberries and the cook would make little tarts for us….Most Sunday evenings a movie was shown by the pool. We sat on the hillside under the stars and enjoyed such fare as "The Circular Staircase" and "Dracula"—leading to many nightmares.

While the Employees Outing Association managed Camp Horne, A.H. Burchfield was the guiding spirit behind the camp. He was instrumental in establishing the original camp for the cash boys, had actively helped find a permanent home for the camp in Emsworth and served as chairman of the Outing Association. Fellow employees called him the "father and big brother of the camp" and the "Guiding Spirit."

During the summer, AHB, as he was affectionately called, lived at the camp with his family in a large wooden lodge called The Burches. Next to the lodge was a tent, the "Waldorf Castoria," that he also used.

AHB was remembered as "chief instigator of some of Camp's most fondly remembered pranks and activities." J.W. McCreary, who succeeded Mr. Burchfield as "Camp Boss," recalled, "from very first camping days until health forced him to give up camp activities [he]…was leader of all kinds of activities…hayrides, trips to ball games, shows, community sings…[he] once took a group of campers out for some fun and deliberately had them arrested and thrown into the Ben Avon 'jug.'" On another occasion, when

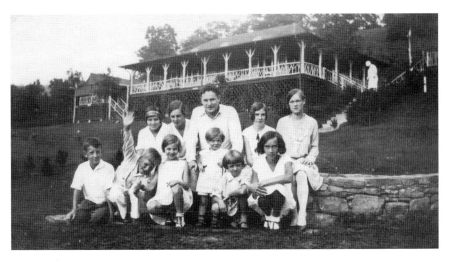

A.H. Burchfield and his wife spent the camping season at The Burches, a permanent building seen behind this group of campers. *Courtesy of Avonworth Historical Society.*

the kitchen staff had the night off for a picnic, AHB dressed up in costume as a Pullman chef while the women cooked dinner. Employees dressed up in blackface with "kinky black wigs" served the food. At the time in the 1920s, the antics were seen as comical rather than insensitive.

Camp season often ended with a Labor Day testimonial to AHB. In 1919, campers pulled him around the camp in a skiff on wheels and gave him a steamer robe and a jacket made from a steamer robe for his upcoming buying trip to Europe. In 1920, they gave him a silver replica of his tent, the "Waldorf Castoria."

In 1937, Camp Horne held a tribute to AHB and named him "Camper No. 1." His health may have already been declining, making camping more difficult. In a *Horne-Pipe* article after his death, a camper remembered, "One of his chief pleasures was to gather a crowd of the little children at Camp on his porch, to entertain them. So many of us remember him as he presided over the old Mess Hall, led the Grand Marches at the dances, and did everything he knew how to foster the spirit of good fellowship and comradeship among all employees. And that's the picture of his we'll cherish in our memories."

During the 1930s, the financial challenges of the Depression affected Camp Horne. The dining hall closed in 1937, and the Corner Store snack shop was enlarged to serve meals to the younger employees who wanted to stay at camp for the summer. The camp itself closed in the summer of

This caricature celebrates "AHB" and his upcoming buying trip to Europe. His sendoff at Camp Horne included gifts from store employees.

1942, and the annual picnic was canceled because tire rationing made it difficult for people to get to camp. Horne's needed to use its tire ration for delivery and couldn't run buses back and forth to camp. Individual car owners often stopped running their cars at all. Camp Horne was opened on weekends for private picnics but closed at dusk because the electricity was turned off for the season.

After the war, the camp reopened. The highlight of its later years was the three-day picnic over the July 4 weekend in 1949 to celebrate the store's centennial. There was a model of the first Horne's store and

The "Picnic of the Century" included a replica of the first Horne's store, where picnickers could have their photos taken.

During the 1949 Picnic of the Century at Camp Horne, two Jeep merry-go-rounds entertained the children.

plywood cutouts of period costumes where employees could pose for photographs. The Horne's Picnic of the Century included games and a diving exhibition at the pool on Saturday, dancing in the afternoon to Slim Bryant and his Wildcats and rides for the children on two Jeep merry-go-rounds, one with Mac the Piano Playing Clown. A Horne's softball team played a team from Allis-Chalmers. That evening, there was more dancing and movies for the kids.

On Sunday afternoon, there was more swimming and a "pop" concert, followed by a sneak preview of a Hollywood film in the evening. Monday was the big day, with more swimming and dancing, a Golden Gloves boxing tournament and fireworks at 9:30 p.m.

By the 1950s, Camp Horne was only open on the weekends for employees who wanted to picnic or use the swimming pool. There seemed to be less employee interest in using the camp, perhaps because so many employees now lived in the suburbs instead of the city. They didn't need a country retreat.

In 1962, Horne's leased the camp to the Avonworth Municipal Authority for use as a public park. When the lease expired, the authority offered to buy the camp. Using Pennsylvania Project 70 funds and federal grants, it was able to buy 119 acres and the existing camp improvements from Horne's. Camp Horne became Accord Park.

Visitors to Accord Park today can still see the original kitchen building and the concrete cellar used as an early refrigerator. Architects who designed new buildings for the park used historic camp buildings for inspiration, so the park retains much of the atmosphere of the old Camp Horne, although many of the open fields are now covered by forest. Children still wade in Lowrie's Run, there are big old shade trees and green grass and families come to picnic on the weekends.

Bibliography

Avonworth Historical Society. 300 Camp Horne Road, Pittsburgh, PA 15202. Folder on Camp Horne and electronic images of the camp.

The Department Store Museum. http://www.thedepartmentstoremuseum. org.

Harris, Leon. *Merchant Princes: An Intimate History of Jewish Families Who Built Great Department Stores.* New York: Harper and Row, 1979.

Howard, Vicki. *From Main Street to Mall: The Rise and Fall of the American Department Store.* Philadelphia: University of Pennsylvania Press, 2015.

Joseph Horne Company Records. MSS 398, Historical Society of Western Pennsylvania Library and Archives Division, John H. Heinz History Center, Pittsburgh, Pennsylvania. Manuscript Boxes 1–122, *Horne-Pipe* Box, Photograph Boxes 1–27.

Pittsburgh Post-Gazette Archives. Accessed November 2017 to June 2018 using search terms "Horne," "Horne's Christmas," "Joseph Horne" and the year where applicable; additional searches for "Camp Horne," "Symphony Gala" and for individual Horne's managers. https://archives. post-gazette.com.

Whittaker, Jan. *Service and Style: How the Department Store Fashioned the Middle Class.* New York: St. Martin's Press, 2006.

About the Author

L etitia Savage published her first article while still in college, a chapter for an engineering book on the effects of oil spills on marine organisms. She continued freelance magazine writing while working as an environmental consultant, primarily on hazardous waste cleanups for the military and the USEPA. In addition to contributing environmental and gardening articles to *Country Journal*, she wrote about horse training and horse keeping for many national horse publications, including *Chronicle of the Horse* and *Horse Illustrated*. After years of magazine writing, Ms. Savage published her first book, on Kaufmann's Department Store in Pittsburgh, for The History Press in 2016. She and her husband live in a pre–Civil War farmhouse that they restored in Sewickley, Pennsylvania. She is often tempted away from writing by gardening and riding, as well as by volunteering as an environmental educator for the local nature center.